D1646407

RELAXATION

Explores the nature of stress and stress-related illnesses and describes the development and use of modern techniques of stress management, with the emphasis on self-help.

RELAXATION
Modern Techniques for Stress Management

by
Sandra Horn
B.Tech.(Hons Psych), Dip.Clin.Psych.

Series Editor

George T. Lewith
MA., M.R.C.G.P., M.R.C.P.

THORSONS PUBLISHING GROUP
Wellingborough, Northamptonshire
Rochester, Vermont

First published May 1986
Second Impression July 1986

British Library Cataloguing in Publication Data

Horn, Sandra
  Relaxation: modern techniques for stress management.
  1. Relaxation
  I. Title
  613.7'9   RA785

  ISBN 0-7225-1187-6

Printed and bound in Great Britain

DEDICATION

For Niall, Eliot, Abigail and Robert

Acknowledgement

I should like to acknowledge my grateful thanks to Dr George Lewith for all his help in the preparation of this book; to Dr Niall Horn for information and assistance with the physiology; to Margaret Course for patiently typing and re-typing (and re-re-typing) the manuscript and for helpful suggestions about the content; and to Heather Unsworth for the funny, wry cartoons which sparkle through the text.

Contents

Foreword

How many times have friends, family or professional advisers told you to relax? It's often an easy thing to say, but may be a very difficult state to achieve. Sometimes the very suggestion to relax starts the tension off again, and too frequently we tend not to see ourselves as tense, irritable and overwrought. This lack of insight may result from our lifestyle and the problems it generates. A whole variety of life events may have increased our levels of stress to a point where further stimuli are destructive rather than constructive. Having the insight to understand these processes within ourselves is the first and probably the most important step in developing a healthy, productive and open view of the world and our relationships. Such insights certainly make us more pleasant companions and workmates.

Sandra Horn writes from a sound basis of experience as a practising clinical psychologist. Her innate clinical abilities shine through the text and provide us with a broad and very practical approach to the vast amount of information available in this general area. Differentiating 'pop' psychology from the techniques that are likely to have a widespread, useful long-term value, is often difficult. She has succeeded in putting together an excellent guide that covers a discussion of stress and its implications, while providing a whole range of techniques that can be used to manage and control the potentially destructive effects of over-stressing ourselves.

The book is written for those qualified in medicine and related areas as well as the interested layman. Some of the ideas discussed are thought-provoking and quite detailed, but the text is not complicated or littered with psychological or psycho-analytical jargon. The insights and suggestions, if taken to heart, could, I am sure, help all of us to deal better with the 1980s and 90s!

GEORGE T. LEWITH
M.A., M.R.C.G.P., M.R.C.P.
Southampton 1986

Introduction

Throughout the history of conventional Western medicine much effort has been expended on diseases caused by micro-organisms. We have advanced a great way in the identification and control (in some cases, eradication) of these diseases.

In general, the more advanced and sophisticated the society, the less its members are prey to the plagues and pestilences of earlier and more primitive times. Modern men and women in the West tend to be well nourished and to live in hygienic surroundings, with access to a range of useful drugs and health services when they are needed. Instead of having to combat the diseases of poverty and dirt, many of us find that we are up against the so-called diseases of affluence. Unfortunately, pills are not the answer to conditions caused by faulty diet, lack of exercise, smoking, alcohol and drug abuse, and stress. All these things require active changes in some aspects of our lives, and it is much harder to make a change in our lives than it is just to take a pill. It is particularly hard when the change involves giving up something that brings immediate comfort and gratification for the promise of being healthier in the future, which is somewhat vague and abstract.

Some unlucky people find the necessity for change thrust upon them as a matter of life and death. For the majority, however, these 'new' diseases will be fought by a long-term process of education and a change in attitudes. The major emphases will be on personal health management and prevention. Like many another old adage, 'prevention is better than cure' has tended to trip lightly over our lips and to disturb our brain processes not at all. We have used such sayings as if they were magic charms; as if merely repeating them is sufficient — no further action needed.

In the matter of health, prevention is surely acknowledged to be better than cure, but it has been much, much harder to implement. Somehow, messages about preventive medicine have been less than convincing. Often, people tend to shy away from taking responsibility for their own health and take refuge in a primitive fatalism — 'when your number comes up, that's it', 'you've got to die of something'. Attempts to use the power of statistics have also, on the whole, been unfruitful. Quoting statistics which link smoking with lung cancer, for example, may be countered with such comments as, 'My uncle smoked forty cigarettes a day and lived to be eighty years old'. The familiar case, the known story, is more powerfully convincing than someone else's table of probabilities. We also seem to fear changing our old habits, such as our usual diet. To deprive ourselves of our habitual

You've got to die of something . . .

comforting foods is simply too hard. Perhaps for the generation which grew up during the deprivations of war such fear is too deep-rooted to be easily overcome. For all these reasons, and no doubt for many others, preventive medicine has been a slow starter.

When the National Health Service was set up it was envisaged that it would concentrate its resources initially on the problems of acute illnesses, and that once these were solved it would primarily be concerned with preventive medicine. In practice, the problems of acute and chronic medical disorders continued to grow with the Health Service, and it is only in very recent years that the cost of failing to put resources into preventive medicine has been counted, and things have begun to change.

One of the most challenging and difficult aspects of preventive medicine is that it puts much of the responsibility for health on to the patient. Many people have grown up with the idea that nearly all illness or disorder happens by mischance — from dental decay to lung disease, it's all a question of bad luck. This sort of thinking fosters feelings of relative helplessness and it goes along with the idea that a

. . . but you could live a little first!

person's responsibility if they are ill is limited to carrying out the doctor's instructions about the pills, and hoping that they work.

It is clear, however, now that much more is known about the role of such things as diet, exercise habits and lifestyle in the onset and progression of many disorders, that the passive swallowing of medicines will, in these cases, be seen as hardly adequate. The active participation of the patient in the management of his life, so as to minimize the chances of developing some disease, or in the control or reversal of some disease processes, is very much in the vanguard of modern medicine and health care. The message that if you are fit you enjoy life more is now being propagated, not by scientists with tables of statistics, but by stars from sport and show business and others outside the conventional health industry: the message is being spread not in hospitals but in the community, in self-help groups, evening classes and clubs. People are beginning to take the initiative for themselves, and things are changing.

1. The Changing Scene in Health Care

As the consumers in the health industry change, so must the suppliers. In medicine and the other healing arts there are moves in the patient-therapist relationship away from the idea of the patient as someone to whom therapeutic things are done by a doctor, nurse or other health care professional.

In my own discipline of clinical psychology, for example, there has been a swing away from primitive behaviourism, which uses a simplistic form of learning based on work with animals. In this form of therapy, behaviour may be changed (or shaped) by rewarding (or reinforcing) desirable responses, and by allowing undesirable responses to be extinguished by not reinforcing them, or sometimes by repeatedly pairing them with unpleasant stimuli. In the past, behaviour such as smoking or alcoholism has been treated by associating it with nausea, or painful electric shock, for example. Although the active co-operation of the patient is usually required in this kind of learning, the therapist is the primary manipulator in the learning process. The more recent development of cognitive psychology, which uses learning in a more conscious way, depends on the therapist and patient working together in a series of problem-solving tasks, which they will have identified together, towards mutually agreed goals. It has this in common with behaviour therapy. Where they differ is that cognitive psychology uses the patient's knowledge, understanding and personal skills as active therapeutic tools. The therapist's skill is in helping the patient to develop coping and managing strategies in the context of a supportive, uncritical, emotionally non-demanding relationship. These qualities in the therapeutic relationship help to free the patient from a tangle of self-critical emotions, so that the task in hand can be the focus of attention. This kind of working relationship can also relieve therapists of the burden of being regarded as superhuman, or in possession of some sort of mystical knowledge or power. It puts them in their right place, i.e. as technical experts such as one might consult to help sort out the car engine, or a legal dispute.

The process of removing the therapist from the pedestal has been slow to come to psychology, and to medicine generally, but it is coming, and it is an essential precursor to successful preventive medicine. It goes hand in hand with more active and responsible participation on the part of patients — or clients, as many health care professionals now prefer to call them.

Changes in Emphasis
The change in the balance of power between therapist and client is one aspect of modern preventive medicine and health care. Another is a more holistic approach to problems. For example, obesity can be, and has been, treated with potent drugs designed to speed up the body's metabolic rate so that surplus energy-producing food is 'burned off' rather than laid down as fat. The modern management of obesity is much more likely to involve an investigation into eating styles and habits, and perhaps such things as the client's self-image and relationships. Obese people may be treated not with drugs at all, but by being put in touch with a psychologist, dietician, or self-help group. Whichever one, or combination of them, clients are helped by, they themselves will be encouraged to take control of the problem. They will be helped to manage their lives in a different way, rather than being the passive recipients of a cure administered by a professional therapist.

This change is not only true of obesity, but of a wide range of long-term chronic or recurrent medical problems such as some forms of migraine, asthma, irritable bowel syndrome, and many others, including so-called neurotic disorders. Many of these disorders will come into the category 'stress-related'.

The Treatment of Stress
In no areas of health care are these changes in emphasis more apparent than in those involved in the treatment of stress disorders and stress-related diseases. These include not just areas traditionally covered by psychiatry, such as anxiety

states, but also a wide range of syndromes across the health spectrum, from reactive depression to psychosomatic illnesses, cardiovascular problems and chronic pain — the list is long.

A large number of disorders have a stress component in their onset and/or progression. Many purely physical problems generate stress, and many life-stresses have a significant effect on the organic body. Prolonged or repeated stress can, in some people, contribute to high blood-pressure, which can in turn be the precursor to such life-threatening events as heart attack or stroke. Modern research also shows that some of the chemicals involved in the immune system, which defends the body against pathogens (disease producing organisms), are suppressed for a while following a stressful experience.

The immune system is extremely complex and not yet fully understood. It carries out a constant surveillance of the body cells and protects them from disease-causing organisms. It is also active in guarding the body from allergy-producing substances, cancers, and from a range of diseases known as auto-immune, in which the immune cells attack the normal tissue of the body. Rheumatoid arthritis is an example of an auto-immune disease.

The immune system can be affected by a variety of things, such as age, nutritional status, drugs, genetic make-up, and so on.[1] Although many of the studies suggesting stress as another factor are scientifically weak, the weight of the evidence favours the idea that psychological and social events affect the functioning of the immune system. Jemmott and Locke have carried out a major review of studies on psychological stress and immunological functioning, and they conclude that the bulk of evidence supports the view that stress is associated with an increased incidence of a variety of diseases and with decreased immuno-competence. However, they also stress that much more investigation needs to be done, and only a few facts are firmly established as yet. A major difficulty in this kind of research is that individual differences in reactions are not well understood and can vary widely. This is also true of the action of our genetic make-up, of bacteria, or unbalanced diet, or many other things affecting our bodies, of course. Individual reactions to these things vary in ways which are not well understood.

Stress does, however, seem to be implicated in certain illnesses or disease states, or states of mind. But merely saying that stress is what precipitates stress-related disorders hardly advances our understanding. Part of the problem is that 'stress' is often used to describe the event causing an upset, as well as the upset itself. Stress comprises events or sequences of events which lead to subjective feelings of distress (tension, fear, anger, frustration, grief) and which also result in some degree of physiological upheaval. The outside events, the uncomfortable emotion, and the physiological response, are all part of the complex. Given the scope for variation between individuals in all parts of the complex, perhaps it should be no surprise that research into stress has generated some lively disagreements — not least about what is cause and what is effect.

For example, a great deal of research has been carried out into the effects of stressful life-events such as bereavement. Hawkins and others[2] with their Schedule of Recent Experiences, and Holmes and Rahé[3] with the Social Readjustment Rating Scale, have pioneered the work. Scales like these use lists of events which have previously been rated in terms of their stress-generating potential by large samples of people. Events range from things like the death of a spouse, at the top end, to committing a minor traffic offence, near the bottom.

Some studies have shown that people with various illnesses or disease states, from depression to cancer, report more distressing life-events in the period before the onset of their problem than do healthy people of a similar age and background. Other studies have failed to demonstrate any such pattern. One problem is that the 'score' quoted against each event on the scale carries with it the assumption that a high- or low-scoring event will have a similar impact for everyone and that the scores can be added up like sums, to give an accumulated stress rating. These assumptions are not true. The 'scores' have been averaged out from a large sample, so that it is true that many people agreed on them, but we still need to know how any one individual felt about the event. Being caught committing a minor traffic offence may be tossed off lightly by one person, but it could be the source of a great deal of shame and anguish to another. Again, while the death of a spouse must always cause distress and major life-changes, it may have a different impact if it is expected after a long-drawn-out illness in an elderly person, than if it is a sudden death from an accident in a young person. Personal factors, then, will modify the impact of life-events. So, of course, will social factors, such as the amount of family support.

It is also apparent that for some groups of people a disaster-prone lifestyle goes hand in hand with a tendency to have a high frequency of distressing life-events; cause and effect then become impossible to separate. Among groups with very high annual frequencies of distressing life-events are heroin addicts and alcoholics. Among groups reporting low frequencies are medical students and pregnant mothers.

The elderly report far fewer distressing life-events than the young. Kasl and others[4] argue from these data that some lifestyles are such that they will generate more stressful life-events than others, and that it is inherent in the life-cycle that some parts of it involve more difficult changes and challenges than others. Kasl also comments that ill people, particularly the depressed, may show a tendency to recall things in a biased way, because their mood is low, which tends to exaggerate their reporting of stressful life-events. This does not negate the value of all such research. But it does suggest that somehow individual variations in lifestyle (including age) need to be allowed for in assessing the significance of stressful events, and that also each individual's experience of stress needs to be looked at, and rated, as there is undoubtedly some variation in what people find stressful, as well as a measure of agreement. Holmes and Rahé report, for example, that during the year following divorce, divorcees have an illness rate which is twelve times that of comparable married people, and ten times more widows and widowers die during the year following the death of their spouse than all others in the same age-group. Statistics such as these strongly suggest the potency of changes involving an exit from one's life as stressors.

However, other events on the Holmes and Rahé scale, such as retirement or moving house, have been studied and no clear health outcome emerges. It can be argued that where the life-event is expected, 'normal' for that part of the life-cycle, and to some extent within the control of the individual, it may not always be stressful. Enforced redundancy in an earlier stage of life, then, would be a stronger stressor than expected retirement at sixty-five. Holmes and Rahé also argue that numbers of such life-events occurring one after the other are likely precursors of disease. The finding that heroin addicts tend to follow the pattern does not necessarily turn the argument on its head. Extreme lifestyles might well show a sequence of self-generating stress events, and then cause and effect become hard to disentangle; but it cannot be argued that stressful life-events are *not* causing further disruption of health from such evidence. The attempt to quantify the stress-generating potential of life-events has been a valuable stimulus to many researchers interested in the cause of a variety of diseases.

Given that there is some disagreement about the precise role of stress in the aetiology of disease — and this will be explored more fully in the next chapter — that there *is* stress, and that it can be damaging, is not in question. But how then to deal with it?

Active Stress Management

A passive pill-taking model of therapy mentioned at the beginning of this chapter might involve the use of drugs to reduce the unpleasant feelings and bodily responses associated with stress. These can sometimes be useful in the short term, where the discomfort produced by those feelings and responses is overwhelming and therefore contributes more stress. However, drugs will not make the stress-producing situation go away. Furthermore, it has been convincingly argued by Dr Peter Tyrer[5] that while tranquillizers can relieve the mood disturbance associated with mental and physical trauma, they may also aid the process of denial, thus making it harder to deal with the roots of the stress. There is also the danger that short-term use may progress to long-term dependence.

Dr Tyrer recommends that 'tranquillisers should only be used if the stress is severe enough to lead to marked changes in behaviour, is unpredicted, and is likely to have a clear beginning and end. . . . Tranquillisers are excellent as first-aid, but much less appropriate as maintenance therapy'. The sort of event that produces such a response will probably be escaped by most of us, and in its severity, unpredictedness and discreteness is unlike the more usual life-stresses that most of us undergo. These more familiar stresses, with their potential toll on our health and well-being, do not need first-aid but management.

One of the difficulties which prevents us from taking our lives in hand and adopting a new approach, such as stress-management, is the strength of habit. Diet has already been mentioned, and it is a good example of the strength of habit. We eat a Sunday roast because we have always eaten it. Examining this practice may reveal that it is in many ways a disaster. It occupies a lot of time to prepare and eat. It breaks up the day. It leaves everyone feeling too full to enjoy the afternoon. It is nutritionally undesirable — too much animal fat and starch. Yet for many families, the mere suggestion that a lighter meal, eaten in the early evening perhaps, would be better, is almost a crime. The Christmas menu is equally sacrosanct. What we eat and when, the patterns in our daily routine, and our habitual modes of behaviour, often have the feel about them that they have been laid down as everlasting and inviolable rules, to be accepted without question. Many habits do, of course, have a valuable function. They give us a sense of identity with others whose behaviour is similar, and a sense of continuity. Such things are not to be tossed aside lightly, and in the main there is no reason why they should be discarded. The need to examine them only comes when the habitual behaviours cause more problems than benefits.

'How I react to stress' is often habitual. Perhaps it is a good habit, involving taking things easy, relaxing, talking it over with a trusted friend, making decisions based on cool logic rather than heated emotion. These are habits worth keeping. On the other hand if the habit involves nail-biting, excess smoking, alcohol intake or eating, screaming, tension, swearing, losing one's temper, disturbed sleep, inward turmoil (even with outward calm), headache, nervous tummy, becoming ill, kicking the cat or snarling at the baby, or any other such non-useful reaction, it is well worth working at changing it.

It is true that old habits die hard, but die they do if they are worked on with sufficient purpose. They may seem to be a part of us, but we can learn to change them. In fact, we can learn to change not just our overt behaviour but the way our bodies react. Stress management at that level is one of the bases of good health care, and it will undoubtedly play an increasing role in preventive medicine, curative and maintenance therapy.

References

1. Jemmott, John B. III and Locke, Steven E. (1984), 'Psychosocial factors, immunologic mediation, and human susceptibility to infectious diseases: how much do we know?' *Psychol. Bull.*, Vol. 95, No. 1, pp. 78–108.

2. Hawkins, N.G., Davies, R. and Holmes, T.H. (1957), 'Evidence of psychosocial factors in the development of pulmonary tuberculosis.' *Amer. Rev. Tuberc. Pulmon. Dis.*, Vol. 75, pp. 768–80.

3. Holmes, T.H. and Rahé, R.H. (1967), 'The Social Readjustment Rating Scale.' *J. Psychosom. Res.*, Vol. 11, pp. 213–18.

4. Kasl, S.V., 'Pursuing the link between stressful life experiences and disease: a time for re-appraisal.' In *Stress Research*, ed. Cary L. Cooper (Wiley, 1983).

5. Tyrer, P.J. (1983), 'The place of tranquillisers in the management of stress.' *J. Psychosom. Res.*, Vol. 27, No. 5, pp. 385–390.

2. Threat and the Autonomic Nervous System

What is Stress?

Stress is a word much bandied about today, not least in the opening pages of this book. Like many such blanket terms it covers a multitude of ills, but often covers them in a threadbare and inadequate way. Stress is clearly more than simply feeling upset or threatened as it can, apparently, cause bodily changes and disorders. This seems maladaptive and yet, at a neurophysiological level, it may be that the early physical responses associated with stress-related disorders have their origins in a perfectly-adapted system which was designed to maximize our chances of survival.

Fight or flight.

In the early history of mankind life was full of physical dangers. Survival often depended on the body's capacity to produce rapidly, and to sustain, an intense burst of physical activity, for fighting or fleeing, or chasing prey.

Equally important was the capacity of the body to return to a steady, energy-conserving state afterwards. These two attributes are mediated by that part of the nervous system known as the autonomic ('self-regulating') system, which is part of modern man's inheritance from those early ancestors. That part of the autonomic nervous system known as parasympathetic is, in general, concerned with growth, repair and the conservation and storage of energy; while the so-called sympathetic part of the system facilitates muscular activity, and can also damp down any process which

Autonomic Nervous System.

interferes with muscular efficiency. For example, it can boost the blood supply to the skeletal muscles, heart and lungs by diverting some of the blood from the deeper organs, like those concerned with digestion. Indulging in a burst of muscular activity, like running for a bus, too soon after eating, gives us unmistakeable signals that in doing so we have caused the process of digestion to be inhibited. The leaden feeling of gastric discomfort is the result of the sympathetic system's activity.

Nerves feeding the sympathetic 'chain' leave the spinal cord in the region of the chest and abdomen. Those forming the parasympathetic system emerge in two groups: one from the cranial region and the other from the lower back. Together they reach organs all over the body.

The whole system consists of a network of nerves which control the smooth muscles of the internal organs and blood vessels, the tiny piloerector muscles which make our hair 'stand on end', and the sweat, salivary, digestive and other glands. Thus it is an extensive part of the peripheral nervous system. It also has important controlling areas in the central nervous system (i.e. brain and spinal cord) and a hormonal system associated with it. In the nerve cells and hormones is a system of internal communication and control of the body which can be localized and specific, or widespread, and can respond to internal and external stimuli.

For example, in low light nervous activity causes relaxation of the iris of the eye by making the tiny radial muscles contract. This is a specific function, localized to those particular muscles. Its purpose is to regulate the amount of light reaching the sensitive retina of the eye. In contrast, the presence in the blood of adrenalin, a hormone released in response to sympathetic activity, has a widespread effect throughout the body and influences muscles, blood vessels, gut, the body's metabolic rate, and many other systems simultaneously and in a massive way. Adrenalin is produced in response to an external stimulus perceived as threatening. (See Table 1 on page 29.)

The Autonomic Nervous System
The autonomic nervous system, with its two complementary parts, is controlled by particular structures in the brain and fed by a series of receptors for such things as temperature,

pain, blood-pressure and body chemistry. Through its central control, it can effect changes in the body in response to external stimuli, producing emotional responses such as fear or anger too. In controlling the vegetative processes of the body, it does not normally need our conscious will to effect changes, although we *can* develop conscious control of many of its functions.

One of the problems faced by modern man is that, although there are still plenty of physical dangers in our environment which require us to run away or stay put and fight, these are few and far between for most of us, most of the time. Of course, some things in our environment are dangerous or destructive. For example, noise of a certain pitch and volume can damage hearing. If we are subjected to such noise, it feels intolerable. We feel agitated, desperate, upset — there is an overwhelming need to shut it out or get away from it. The extremes of heat or cold, or pain, can also make us feel that sense of urgency or agitation. Such a feeling of stress has obvious survival value: it involves a burst of energy designed to make us seek to change things quickly — to move away fast from the noise, the heat, the cold, the thing that is hurting us. We need not only the sense of urgency but the feeling of discomfort and agitation to make us act with speed, before damage is done. The signal 'danger' produces a fast physiological reaction in us, mediated by the autonomic nervous system, involving the release of adrenalin.

Nowadays we are likely to feel the stress and the sense of urgency and danger in situations which do *not* demand an

Fight or flight won't help you.

intense burst of physical activity, but the autonomic nervous system still responds to threat by preparing us for it. Modern stresses are much more likely to impinge on us in the form of, say, the close proximity of fast-moving traffic, or unexpected bad news, or the anticipation of an angry quarrel. In such cases intense bursts of sympathetic activity, with its accompanying subjective feelings of fear, anger, agitation, may be far from helpful. The massive 'threat' or stress response surges through the body, but has, in a sense, nowhere to go.

Table 1

The Autonomic Nervous System

SYMPATHETIC gives activation for violent activity, stress reaction, ('fight or flight'); e.g. sympathetic activity tends to:

increase
  heart-rate and force of contraction
  cardiac output
  blood-pressure
  muscle blood flow
  sweating
  basal metabolic rate and glycogen breakdown (for energy release)
  hair erection
  rate of adrenalin release

while *decreasing*
  most gland secretions (digestion, salivation, etc.)
  blood flow through skin, gut, etc.
  motility and tone in stomach and intestine, etc.

PARASYMPATHETIC prepares body for rest and recovery, it:

increases
  gland secretions
  gut mobility
  glycogen synthesis (energy store)

decreases
  heart-rate
  blood-pressure
  cardiac output, etc.

Repeated exposure to experiences such as these can cause changes in the way the autonomic nervous system functions, so that we become sensitized and the response will fire off more readily than before. When this firing of the autonomic nervous system is triggered repeatedly by a given set of circumstances, it can happen that other things associated with the event can also in time become triggers. For example, it is not uncommon for people who have had very unpleasant experiences in a particular place to feel anxious and upset in similar places. A student who had become very distressed by being jammed into the middle of a mass of people in an underground train, and had felt that it was hard to breathe, went on to have similar panicky feelings in other enclosed, hot places, like his car when it was held up in a traffic jam. Another, older man, who had been trapped in a lift, later began to feel panicky in telephone booths, and ultimately could not sit in his own living-room with the door shut. A sensitized autonomic system can make us vulnerable.

Anyone unlucky enough to have remained in a state of autonomic arousal for any length of time will know that all sorts of trivial events can impinge upon us like bombshells while we are in that state. A distant door slamming, or a car backfiring in the street outside, can make us 'jump out of our skin'. It is exhausting and unpleasant, and is often accompanied by poor sleep and depressed appetite.

Fortunately, for most of us, such experiences are uncommon enough that the system can settle back down to normal functioning. It is only when the experience is extremely upsetting, or when the system is repeatedly triggered by events, so that the 'emergency' state is not allowed to dissipate naturally and let the body return to its steady level of functioning, that the possibilities of physical or emotional disorder become enhanced.

This is, however, by no means the whole story of stress. The autonomic nervous system governs the vegetative functions of the body, with the sympathetic and parasympathetic systems in a dynamic balance, constantly changing throughout the sleeping and waking cycle. The body's organs and their functions are also part of that dynamic balancing act. Each will have its own local balance between parasympathetic and sympathetic control. For example, a situation that we experience as embarrassing may cause the heart-rate to increase (sympathetic), while the skin blood vessels dilate, producing a blush (parasympathetic). The autonomic nervous system manages the vegetative body processes while responding to stimuli engendering fear, anger, interest, sexual attraction, and so on.

Emotions and Illness

The delicate balancing act can be thrown into disorder not only by the occasional drama of the fight or flight syndrome, from which, as we have seen, it usually recovers rapidly, but by a range of distressing emotional experiences. Just as all of us will inevitably be exposed to threat from time to time, so will we feel anger, grief, frustration. Most of the situations engendering these feelings will resolve in a reasonable time, and the emotions will fade too. However, this is clearly not always the case. Grief which remains unresolved because something in the external situation, or something in the grieving person, prevents that resolution, can shade into depression. Depression is characterized not only by a sad, helpless, hopeless emotional state, but by vegetative disturbances as well. Appetite, gut motility, the sleeping and waking cycle and energy levels may all be disordered.

Thus a sequence of events arising from external circumstances, and having a long-term effect on normal emotional reactivity, can end by disturbing the basic bodily functions. Exactly how these changes take place is not fully understood, but it appears to involve changes in the balance between message-transmitting chemicals in the brain (neurotransmitters). These chemical changes will, of course, act in the context of individual differences in constitution and circumstance, so that one person may have a depressed appetite, sleep a lot and be low in energy; another may feel agitated, eat excessively and sleep poorly.

Similarly, fear, rage or tension, when prolonged or repeatedly triggered, can be associated with chronic increases in blood-pressure, the release of fatty acids such as cholesterol into the bloodstream, or changes in acid levels in the stomach, or the levels of other chemicals in the voluntary muscles or blood. Where circumstances and constitutional factors allow, these changes can become the precursors of serious disease.

Pain as a Stressor

Another cause of psychological and physiological stress is pain. Acute pain produces the sense of urgency and distress and autonomic arousal, associated with the signal 'danger'. The danger in this case is the onset of tissue damage if the situation is not changed rapidly. Snatching a limb back from a source of heat, or from a sharp object which is penetrating the skin, are examples of the use of the triggering system. This kind of pain is usually short-lived, and allows the return to a steady resting state (homoeostasis) very quickly.

Chronic pain, however, is another story. It is not always a symptom of disease or injury, although it can be. It can persist after injured tissues have healed and it can occur spontaneously. When pain is the sequel to disease or injury, it may be more distressing and debilitating than its original cause. It is a potent stressor, with the physiological, cognitive, emotional and behavioural concomitants seen in other stress-producing states. Just like an unresolved grief or frustration, chronic pain tends to focus the mind on itself, inhibiting normal thought, emotion and behaviour, and fostering the same feelings of helplessness and lack of control over the environment.

Although pain is felt by any normal organism, individual reactions to it differ, and the amount of distress and disruption it causes is a very personal thing. The actual expression of pain is also partly culturally and socially determined: children may cry, adults may be frowned upon for doing so. Stoicism is favoured in some cultures; screaming in others. All these factors affect the stress-producing potential of pain to some degree, but in any individual in any culture it is a basic source of stress.

Stress and Personal Illness

There is a substantial and ever-increasing body of literature concerned with the role of stress in personal illness. However, there are a number of problems involved in teasing out all the factors in stress-related diseases.

First, such things as the resting state (homoeostasis) and the trigger point of the autonomic nervous system seem to be set at different levels in different people. It is not possible to say with absolute certainty whether these differences are genetically determined, or the result of early experiences, but they are part of one's characteristic way of reacting and are present very early on in life. Thus an event producing a full blown 'fight or flight' response in one person may affect another very little, or not at all.

It is commonly believed, and there is scientific evidence to back it up, that those people with more reactive autonomic nervous systems are prone to a range of disorders such as anxiety states, minor illnesses such as headaches and gastric upsets, psychosomatic disorders and some physical illnesses. A recently reported American study showed that 'type A' behaviour — that is an over-tense, competitive, easily-aroused to hostility, urgent way of behaving — can be a significant factor in recurrent heart attacks, for example. In a sample of 800 men who had suffered heart attacks, those who showed characteristic 'type A' behaviour were identified. Results demonstrated that those who received psychological guidance aimed at teaching them to slow down and relax were much less prone to recurrences of heart attack than those who received only the traditional forms of counselling about diet, exercise and smoking. Until now 'type A' behaviour has been regarded as a risk factor in heart attacks, but secondary to such things as high blood-pressure and blood fatty acid levels. Fortunately, although we may have been born with or acquired a tension-prone behaviour pattern, it is possible to learn to modify it, as this book seeks to demonstrate.

Secondly, apart from individual differences in reactivity, the experience of stress can vary in another way. Although there are some environmental events which are felt as stressful by almost everyone, to some degree, such as a sudden very loud noise or a pain-causing stimulus, psychological stressors are not always so widely shared. Many of us have the image of a jet-setting, high-living businessman as a prime candidate for a gastric ulcer or nervous breakdown, but this can hardly be true of all, or even most, such people. Many manage the lifestyle with equanimity, or seem to thrive on it.

We seem to have 'drives' for succeeding in such things as business, sport, home-making, close personal relationships, and so on. Each of these drives will be present in a more or less substantial degree in each of us, as a result of the complex interplay between our genetic inheritance and life-chances and experiences. A strong drive for achievement in a given field can act like hunger or thirst: it directs our behaviour, urgently, to satisfy it. Left unsatisfied, we feel anxious, frustrated, tense. Our mythical jet-setting businessman who thrives on his lifestyle is fulfilling such a need. To those of us without similar needs his life may appear stressful, but he would be more stressed if he could not respond to his chosen challenges. Drives such as these are uniquely personal, and are often a source of amazement to those of us with different needs. How often one of us says of someone 'I couldn't live like that', when that person lives like that very well indeed because they are fulfilled by their lifestyle.

Thirdly, although the emotions usually associated with the upsurge of adrenalin are agitation, fear or anger, which are commonly experienced as unpleasant, some people feel an enjoyable kind of excitement in apparently dangerous

Fear can be fun?

situations and actively seek them out for that reason. Parachute jumping, pot-holing and rock-climbing all spring to mind and there are numerous other examples. A whole section of the fairground industry prospers on scaring people in roller-coaster rides and ghost-trains, as do the horror film and book industries. The very sharpening of visual and auditory acuity, so essential to our hunter ancestors in fight or flight situations, can be experienced by their modern counterparts voluntarily, in leisure activities. The heightened perceptual awareness feels good and is enhanced by the excitement of the heart pounding, dry mouth and prickling of the skin as the autonomic nervous system 'fires off'. An ancient mechanism designed for stark survival can be triggered for fun.

It is clear, then, that in order to be stressful the events pertaining to physiological arousal have to be in some way punishing, frustrating or overwhelming (as when so many new events crowd in that they cannot all be dealt with). In addition, the events must be of such a nature that they repeatedly trigger arousal or do not allow the emergency state to dissipate rapidly again. Stress is a composite of personal, social and physiological upheaval.

Selye[1] has put forward a descriptive model of stress, with four basic variations. He points out the importance of learning to recognize overstress (hyperstress) when we have exceeded the limits of our adaptability, or understress (hypostress) brought about by boredom, lack of self-realization, physical immobility, or sensory deprivation. He talks of those unpleasant or difficult situations we sometimes need to go through in order to attain an ultimate success or fulfilment, 'good stress' (eustress) and contrasts it with bad stress (distress) which is damaging. From his descriptive model he has developed a code of conduct, the point of which is to master stress rather than abolish it. 'It is a matter of choosing, not an undemanding lifestyle, but a eustressfully rather than a distressfully demanding one.'

In a somewhat similar vein, Caplan[2] has evolved, from French's work, 'person-environment fit theory'. The theory involves the notion of two types of fit: needs-supplies fit and abilities-demands fit, each measured in terms of the properties of the person and the environment. The needs and values of the person fit to a greater or lesser degree with the supplies and opportunities in the environment. For example, people vary in their need to achieve a certain level in their job, and the environment varies in the extent to which it provides opportunities to do so. Where the fit between the two is poor 'strain' results. Then there is the fit between the demands of the environment, and the ability of the person to meet the demands. Again, a poor fit leads to strain. Strain (stress) can lead to illness. The model also involves elements of accurate self-assessment, and contact with reality, on the part of the person, and these elements will help to determine the degree of fit.

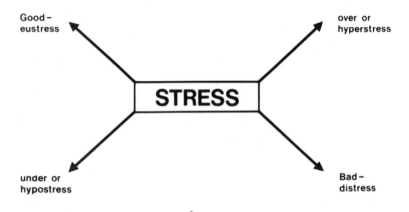

Selye's descriptive model.

Stress Research

Descriptive models such as these — and there are many — are interesting when contemplating the causes of stress in one's life; they can therefore sometimes help in deciding on courses of action, if the options to do so are open. On another level, some day-to-day stresses resulting in autonomic arousal have been modelled in laboratory studies. These, too, have their uses in helping us to understand more about the factors which combine to turn autonomic arousal into stress.

In one such study, for example, subjects were set paper-and-pencil problems to solve. This sort of task usually involves some degree of autonomic arousal — enough to provide interest and energy. It is the same sort of excitement that actors, athletes, and similar others, seem to need to push them on. Then, however, further problems were set which could not be solved, although the subjects were unaware of it. They were working against the clock, and failure to complete the tasks resulted in mild, but painful, electric shock. (More subtle studies have shown that pain itself is not necessary; the mere anticipation of pain is a potent stress-producer.) Similar tasks, such as being set a problem to solve in an impossibly short time, or being given a task to complete in a group where one member of the group was a 'plant' whose job was to create conflict, have also been used. All such situations produced not only subjective feelings of distress, but increases in blood-pressure, sweat production and respiratory rate. They also produced changes suggestive of arousal in the electro-encephalogram (E.E.G.).

The E.E.G. consists of the very small electrical signals (a few hundred-thousandths of a volt) generated by cells in the brain. These signals can be picked up by electrodes placed on the scalp and are usually displayed as tracings on a pen-recorder or may be transmitted through a visual display unit.

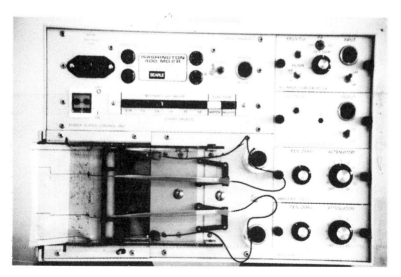

A polygraph, used to measure physiological responses in stress research.

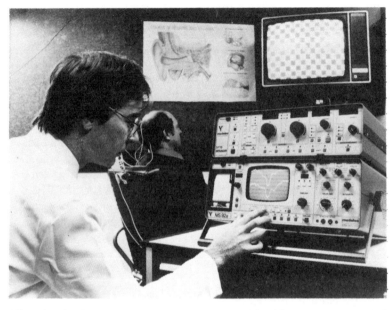

The checked pattern is generating particular brain waves (visual evoked potentials) which are being displayed on the small screen. (Photograph courtesy of Medelec Ltd.)

The overlying parts of the brain (cerebral cortex) contain millions of large nerve cells, each of which is normally producing electrical signals in response to input from other parts of the brain. These signals are not synchronized, and when the brain is active they tend to cancel each other out and produce a low-voltage E.E.G. with no clear pattern. However, when the level of arousal decreases the nerve cells tend to become synchronized and the E.E.G. develops larger and slower wave forms. In relaxation, the E.E.G. tends to display a wave form with a frequency of about ten cycles per second (or 10 hertz) especially over the back of the head. This pattern of waves is known as the alpha rhythm and it disappears on arousal.

For example if a relaxed subject is asked to perform some mental arithmetic, the E.E.G. becomes small, fast and desynchronized. Sleep produces even larger and slower waves (delta), which disappear during dreaming. In general, a relaxed or sleepy brain shows large, slow and synchronized electrical activity, while an alert, working brain shows small, random, fast activity. The E.E.G. can therefore be used to indicate the level of arousal, especially when coupled with measures of autonomic nervous system activity, such as heart-rate and blood-pressure.

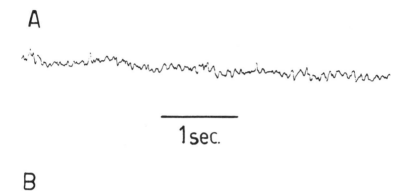

A

1 sec.

B

A : eyes closed, relaxed

B : eyes open, alert

E.E.G. pen-trace recording.

In the studies mentioned, E.E.G. changes suggestive of arousal and changes in the steady rhythm of the heart occurred at times when the subjects' performance on the tasks became less efficient. The suggestion that we are unable to think so clearly when the autonomic nervous system is over-aroused is confirmed by everyday experience. An American study[3] has also shown it to be a particular problem in the elderly and that poor performance on some intellectual tasks, which is often attributed to general deterioration of the central nervous system, can be improved by chemically blocking the effects of adrenalin, or by allowing subjects to take as much time as they need, thus reducing the element of stress produced by pressure of time.

Experiments such as these have parallels in difficult human situations. Problems which inherently cannot be solved, where failure to solve them has bad results, are not only found as paper-and-pencil laboratory tests, but in many interpersonal relationships. For example, a devoted daughter nursing her elderly invalid mother at home may find her life becoming constricted and unhappy, but on the other hand she may feel that the guilt and distress which would come with putting her mother in a nursing home would be as bad or worse. Situations with no way out and no satisfactory solution, only a choice between equally disagreeable alternatives, can be potent stress-generators and the precursors of disease.

Results from laboratory studies are echoed by larger-scale work, pioneered by such workers as Paykel[4] and Holmes and Rahé,[5] mentioned in Chapter 1, on the effects of stressful life-events on health. Holmes and Rahé compiled a list of life-events, such as moving house, retirement, bereavement, changing one's job, and asked a large number of people from several different cultures to rate them for the amount of discontinuity and need for adjustment they would cause. They found significant levels of agreement across cultures.

Table 2

The Holmes and Rahé Social Readjustment Scale

	Life event	*Mean adjustment value*
1.	Death of a spouse	100
2.	Divorce	73
3.	Marital separation from mate	65
4.	Detention in jail or other institution	63
5.	Death of a close family member	63
6.	Major personal injury or illness	53
7.	Marriage	50
8.	Being fired at work	47
9.	Marital reconciliation with mate	45
10.	Retirement from work	45
11.	Major change in the health or behaviour of a family member	44

	Life event	Mean adjustment value
12.	Pregnancy	40
13.	Sexual difficulties	39
14.	Gaining a new family member (e.g. through birth, adoption, elderly relative moving in, etc.)	39
15.	Major business readjustment (e.g. merger, reorganization, bankruptcy, etc.)	39
16.	Major change in financial state (e.g. a lot worse off or a lot better off than usual)	38
17.	Death of a close friend	37
18.	Changing to a different line of work	36
19.	Major change in the number of arguments with spouse (e.g. a lot more or a lot less than usual, regarding childbearing, personal habits, etc.)	35
20.	Taking a mortgage greater than £15,000 (e.g. purchasing a home, business, etc.)	31
21.	Foreclosure on a mortgage or loan	30
22.	Major change in responsibilities at work (e.g. promotion, demotion, lateral transfer)	29
23.	Son or daughter leaving home (e.g. marriage, attending college, etc.)	29
24.	In-law troubles	29
25.	Outstanding personal achievement	28
26.	Wife beginning or ceasing work outside the home	26
27.	Beginning or ceasing formal schooling	26
28.	Major change in living conditions (e.g. building a new home, remodelling, deterioration of home or neighbourhood)	25

Life event	Mean adjustment value
29. Revision of personal habits (dress, manners, associations, etc.)	24
30. Trouble with the boss	23
31. Major change in working hours or conditions	20
32. Change in residence	20
33. Changing to a new school	20
34. Major change in usual type and/or amount of recreation	19
35. Major change in church activities (e.g. a lot more or a lot less than usual)	19
36. Major change in social activities (e.g. clubs, dancing, movies, visiting, etc.)	18
37. Taking on a mortgage or loan of less than £15,000 (e.g. purchasing a car, TV, freezer, etc.)	17
38. Major change in sleeping habits (a lot more or a lot less sleep, or change in part of day when asleep)	16
39. Major change in number of family get-togethers (e.g. a lot more or a lot less than usual)	15
40. Major change in eating habits (a lot more or a lot less food intake, or very different meal hours or surroundings)	15
41. Vacation	13
42. Christmas	12
43. Minor violations of the law (e.g. traffic tickets, jaywalking, disturbing the peace, etc.)	11

Note that not all items on the scale are inherently negative. Marriage, for example, is not a negative change for many people, but it does bring about a period of adaptation and uncertainty — an awareness of a discontinuity in one's life and a need to produce new behaviours.

The events considered most distressing are those involving an exit or loss from one's life, such as bereavement, divorce, loss of a job; and where the changes associated with the event are undesirable, sudden and unplanned, and involve a great deal of rapid adjustment to a new kind of life. There is some evidence that such life-events are more common in the three to six months preceding certain illnesses, such as heart disease, and some minor physical complaints and can increase one's accident proneness; they are implicated in some episodes of depressive breakdown, anxiety states and suicide. Other studies have failed to find any correlation but, as discussed in Chapter 1, there are many problems with the methods of research into such life-events. It is clear that the probability remains high, notwithstanding the difficulties inherent in this particular way of measuring them. American studies have shown, for example, that people who have been through the trauma of divorce or marital separation have a significantly increased chance of developing diseases, such as those mentioned, when compared with similar people who are not separated. The increased risk is comparable to that of smokers developing lung cancer, as against non-smokers.

Although a temporal relationship between life-events and disorders of various kinds has been established, the correlation between the two is far from perfect. Other factors are at work, which can influence the outcome of life-events. Some of these are personal, such as the more-or-less reactive temperament already mentioned; practical intelligence is another example. Some of these factors are social, such as the degree to which there is a network of care and support available. It seems that all the stress-producing events mentioned, whether produced in the laboratory or observed in real life, are destructive because they overturn the normal, predictable pattern of events which enables us to exert some control over our lives. We need to feel that we can manage a situation, whether it is a paper-and-pencil test or a human relationship. Take that away and replace it with a period of uncertainty or the anticipation of failure or pain, while at the same time blocking the exits, and there is a recipe for physiological and emotional turmoil leading to disease and disorder. Nothing can protect us all from meeting such situations, but we can learn to manage them — beginning at the physiological level.

The fact that we need to learn to manage stressful situations is underlined by a recent study in which it is claimed that short-term stress-related illnesses are estimated to cost Britain £55 million a year in National Insurance and Social Security payments alone. The financial cost reflects the human cost, and it is clear that revenues of this order of magnitude are not lost by a few frail individuals taking time off with mild anxiety states. Stress-related illnesses are widespread and no respecters of occupational status. Some organizations are acknowledging the problem and have developed programmes to combat stress. These include stress-awareness training, keep fit classes, counselling and sabbaticals as a way of helping employees develop a wider range of skills and broaden their knowledge. Firms involved in this kind of constructive thinking are using self-help techniques of stress management for their staff. They could usefully add classes in stress-control at the autonomic level.

Techniques designed to reduce the reactivity of the autonomic nervous system, once learned and practised successfully, can reduce blood-pressure, the rate of fatty acid release into the bloodstream, and other emergency reactions. They can also reduce the subjective feelings of distress, and enable a calm and rational approach to be taken to stress-producing problems. None is a cure-all. Like all therapeutic techniques they have a finite range of application, but within that range they are valuable tools in preventive and curative therapy. The following is an example.

A fifty-five year old teacher, in an educational establishment which had undergone a lot of fundamental changes in its teaching philosophy and practice in a short space of time, had become very tense in trying to adapt to the changes. Her resting pulse rate was over 90 per minute, and she was taking large amounts of tranquillizing drugs, and was suffering from pains in the neck and head and insomnia. It was hard for her to continue working. She was given a course of relaxation training and in the space of three months was able to reduce the drugs. Her sleep pattern improved and she became free of pain. Her resting pulse rate dropped to below 80. Because she was more in command of herself she was able to question some of the teaching practices she had found particularly unacceptable, and succeeded in getting some of them changed. Changing her reaction to external stresses took time and effort, but enabled her to work efficiently, reduce her drugs and become fitter. Once she had learned to manage and change her reactions to stress, she could then tackle its external source. That is the nub of stress management: first to modify one's own reactions to external stresses, then to take a calm look at the external source of stress and see how it could be changed.

References

1. Selye, H., The Stress Concept, in *Stress Research: Issues for the Eighties* ed. Cary L. Cooper (Wiley, 1983).
2. Caplan, Robert D., Person-Environment Fit, in Cooper, *op. cit.*
3. Eisdorfer, C., Nowlin, J. and Wilkie, F., (1970) 'Improvement of learning in the aged by modification of automatic nervous system activity.' *Science*, Vol. 170: 1327–1329.
4. Paykel, E.S., (1983), 'Methodological aspects of life events research.' *J. Psychosom. Res.*, Vol. 27, No. 5: 341–352.
5. Holmes, T.H. and Rahé, R.H., (1967), 'The social readjustment rating scale.' *J. Psychosom. Res.*, 11, pp. 213–218.

3. Biofeedback

At the physiological level, a significant difficulty in learning the skills involved in stress management is that we are often trying to modify things we cannot see, hear, smell or feel. In the acquisition of any skill we need to know what we are doing and to have knowledge of the results of our actions. Such knowledge tells us when and how to adjust our behaviour so that we keep on the right road to our goal. Without it we cannot act purposefully.

But many of the physiological concomitants of stress are 'silent'. That is, we cannot feel high blood-pressure or excess fatty acids entering the bloodstream; they produce no recognizable signals for us to identify. Of the stress reactions we *can* feel, such as increased muscle tension, most only intrude upon our consciousness as they get towards the peak of their intensity; we do not usually notice the build-up. Driving a car in difficult or frustrating conditions, like crawling in city traffic, for example, may ultimately result in painful arms and shoulders from increased muscle tension; but we don't notice the tension until it hurts, which is usually too late on in its development. In addition, as we have seen from earlier chapters, such reactions are governed by the autonomic or self-regulating part of the nervous system, and are not usually under our conscious control. Thus we have a set of physiological responses to stress which are self-governing, and either silent or only recognized at peaks of intensity. How is it possible to learn to manage such a system?

Pavlov, the Russian behavioural scientist, showed that conditioning of physiological responses could take place. In his classic experiments with dogs he used the innate response of salivating at the sight of food. When the food was repeatedly paired with the ringing of a bell, the dogs 'learned' to salivate when the bell rang, even when no food was present. The physiological response was triggered by a new stimulus. This demonstrates that an automatic piece of behaviour, not normally under the control of the will, can be manipulated or conditioned.

Later B.F. Skinner, an American behavioural psychologist, established some of the fundamental rules of learning. He showed that behaviour can be shaped or changed by its immediate consequences. If, for example, an animal was rewarded with a small amount of food when it performed a certain act, such as pressing a bar, the incidence of bar-pressing increased, while other unrelated forms of behaviour lessened. The reward had to follow the behaviour immediately in order to reinforce it, and did not have to be given for each and every press of the bar. The animal would go on bar-pressing longest for intermittent reward.

The expectation of reward has a powerful effect on behaviour.

These psychological fundamentals (immediate and intermittent reward) are the principles on which the fortunes of fruit-machine manufacturers are founded. Skinner also showed that the behaviour would cease ('extinguish') if no reward was forthcoming. The best rewards tended to be things which reduced a state of need or drive — such as food to reduce hunger or water to reduce thirst. Later work showed that the opportunity to escape from something unpleasant or painful could also act as a reward; fear, it seems, also acts as a drive, and behaviour which results in its reduction is thus reinforced. This kind of behavioural change is called operant conditioning.

Autonomic Conditioning

The manipulations demonstrated by Pavlov are known as classical conditioning. Then in the 1960s N.E. Miller[1] and his associates began a series of experiments which demonstrated that the autonomic nervous system could also undergo conditioning.

In early experiments, groups of rats were rewarded for increases or decreases in heart-rate. This learning was accomplished by first rewarding small random changes in the desired direction; when the conditioned change became regular, the animal was rewarded for larger and larger deviations from the baseline.

Miller and his colleagues went on to demonstrate the same principle of rewards for increases producing reliable increases, and rewards for decreases producing reliable decreases, for a range of autonomic functions such as blood-pressure, vaso-motor* responses, rate of urine formation by the kidney, rate of secretion of saliva and rate of intestinal contractions. Further work on man, carried out by Miller and his associates, and Shapiro[2] and his group, and many other scientists since, have shown similarly encouraging results. For example, results of one study are shown diagrammatically on page 49.

In this case the reward was simply a tone sounded whenever there was a change in the desired direction. The knowledge of results, mentioned earlier as an essential in learning, also itself acts as reward or reinforcer, as it signals success. This work established the principles of biofeedback:

1) The use of operant conditioning of autonomic responses, similar to classical conditioning of voluntary responses;

* Changes in the diameter of blood vessels and hence the rate of blood-flow through them.

2) Knowledge of desired results as a reinforcer;
3) The use of instrumentation to signal otherwise silent changes back to the subject in a clear and vivid way.

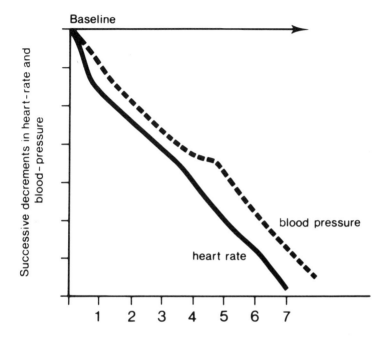

Diagram of results from 4 groups of subjects asked to reduce blood-pressure and heart-rate, over 7 blocks of trials.

So far so good. This pioneering work laid the foundation for the treatment of a variety of conditions such as high blood-pressure, irregularities in cardiac rhythm and output, tension headaches, migraine, and so on. No drugs are used, and therefore there are no problems with side-effects. However, some important points need to be considered, as they do with any new therapeutic technique.

1. It is known that the response to any attempt at therapeutic intervention contains a component known as the placebo effect (placebo: Latin 'I please'). That is, the mere expectation of help often produces a result in the desired direction. For this reason, new drugs are usually tested in

trials where some of the participants receive an inactive compound, some the new drug. They do not know which is which. It is characteristic of such trials that some participants will obtain good results from the inactive drug or placebo. Results from the new drug must be better than those from the placebo alone if it is to prove its effectiveness. It is important to remember that the active drug will have a placebo component too, and it must be demonstrated that it has something more than that.

The placebo effect is present not only in drugs but in procedures as well and its strength can vary according to such things as the enthusiasm of the therapist, and the impressiveness of the procedure. Electronic gadgetry will usually enhance the placebo effect. Some conditions are more susceptible to placebo than others, as are some people. The effect is usually transitory. Neil Miller, writing in the New England Journal of Medicine,[3] comments on one study which concluded that training to warm the hands relieves migraine headache — 'but they had neither a control group nor a long-term follow-up observation — deficiencies that need correction because headaches are notoriously subject to placebo effects and transient fluctuations'. He also draws attention to a study designed to evaluate anti-hypertensive drugs, where 'the placebo medication produced effects that progressively increased for seven weeks, resulting on the average in a decrease of 25 (mm Hg) in systolic and 15 (mm Hg) in diastolic blood pressure.' (*Note:* Blood-pressure is measured in a representative blood vessel, usually in the upper arm. Like the pressure in a barometer, it is measured by how much it can move a standard column of mercury (mm Hg). It is expressed as systolic pressure/diastolic pressure where systolic is the peak pressure in the arteries produced by the ventricles of the heart during contraction; and diastolic is the level that the pressure in the arteries falls to when the heart is not contracting. Thus it is an indirect measure of the amount of work the heart has to do in pumping the blood around the body. High blood-pressure is an extra strain on the heart and is associated with an increased risk of stroke. Blood-pressure, like the other functions mediated by the autonomic nervous system, is labile, i.e. it fluctuates. It goes up when the extra work is required of the heart because of physical exertion in the body, and as a reaction to perceived threat. This can make it difficult to get a reliable baseline. Blood-pressure is usually taken in someone who has been resting for several minutes. Its resting level is the important thing: if that is high, the implication is that the strain on the heart is chronic and excessive.)

These studies show how powerful the placebo effect can be and how easy it is to forward extravagant claims for treatments, where proper experimental controls have been neglected. These points need to be borne in mind not only in considering biofeedback, but all the techniques covered in this book. Fortunately, in each case there are reports of carefully-controlled trials which give support to the usefulness of the methods, within appropriate limits.

2. Any technique is of extremely limited use if it works under laboratory conditions but its effects fade rapidly thereafter. The long-term effects need to be established.

3. The mechanism underlying the technique should have an adequate explanatory model, so that the limits of what it can do can be explored and modifications can be made where necessary. The early work on animals suggested that operant conditioning of the autonomic nervous system was an appropriate model, and indeed it clearly is the basis of biofeedback. However, when biofeedback is carried out on man, the importance of cognition (intellect) cannot be ignored, as it appears that man can alter his internal state in a variety of ways by contemplation. For example, it sometimes is possible to become deeply relaxed and to reduce muscle tension, blood-pressure, heart-rate and output, and effect changes in E.E.G. (brain wave patterns) by thinking about something peaceful, or by the silent repetition of a syllable. Similarly, we can enter into a 'fight or flight' response by calling to mind a frightening or dangerous situation we were once in, or even by imagining one we have never experienced in real life.

Schwartz (1975)[4] suggests that this centrally-controlled response involves a whole pattern of metabolic changes, whereas some of the work on biofeedback demonstrates changes in one response only, such as heart-rate or blood-pressure, while the unconditioned responses remain unchanged. In the management of stress and stress-related conditions, the numerous scientific studies on biofeedback in the last twenty years or so vary widely in approach, but there is an overall impression that the relaxation response enhances biofeedback training. The weight of support is behind the idea of central or cognitive control as a major component of autonomic conditioning, although some studies have demonstrated simple conditioning of certain muscular patterns.

Numerous studies have been carried out on the use of biofeedback. The following account represents a sample of those studies relevant to the topic of stress and stress-related disease. It is a broad, representative view of the scope of such work, rather than an exhaustive review.

Electromyography Biofeedback
When muscles contract and relax, the information produced can be transmitted through electrodes on the skin, recorded, and displayed, usually as a pen-tracing. This is known as electromyography (or EMG). The record can also be fed back to the person undergoing EMG, as a tone which changes in pitch with tension/relaxation of the muscles.

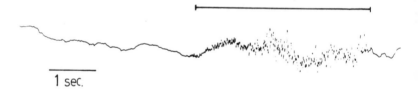

1 sec.

Background muscle activity – progressively increasing muscle tension.

Electromyography

This technique has been used in biofeedback training in a number of conditions. Signals about tension and relaxation have been recorded from the frontalis muscles of the forehead, for example, for the treatment of some types of headache related to stress or tension.

These tension headaches may be unilateral or bilateral and may occur anywhere on the head. They are usually, but not

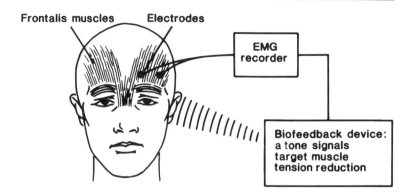

**Muscle relaxation is fed back as an
auditory signal when target level is reached**

E M G biofeedback.

invariably, gradual in onset, and can last for a few hours or days or weeks. The pain is often described as band-like, and it may have a steady intensity or may wax and wane. It is assumed that some sort of psychological stress causes increased tension in muscles in the scalp, face or perhaps neck, which in turn leads to pain. If this is indeed the case, then EMG biofeedback aimed at tension reduction should banish the pain and should be a useful pain-controlling strategy for those who suffer recurrent headache. In studies where some subjects were taught to achieve lowered muscle tension by EMG biofeedback and some were given no treatment, most of them appear to demonstrate the superiority of biofeedback over no treatment. Unfortunately, as we have seen, the placebo effect is not controlled for in such studies, and results are therefore suspect.

When the placebo effect is controlled, by such devices as using true biofeedback for one group and false biofeedback for the other (control) group, or giving the control group inactive 'muscle relaxing pills' or playing various tones or clicks to them as 'relaxation aids', in general, biofeedback produced more positive results (i.e. decreases in headache frequency and/or medication needs) at follow-up. However, other studies have failed to find a difference between the experimental and control groups. In one study, the biofeedback group received seven EMG training sessions; the control group had seven 'meditation' sessions where they were asked to concentrate on various sensations in their hands, arms or body and to imagine some ordinary situations such as sewing on buttons. Immediately after the training sessions, and at follow-up, headache frequency, intensity and duration were recorded from the subjects' accounts. No reliable differences were found between the groups. This was in spite of the fact that the biofeedback group had succeeded in lowering frontalis muscle tension to a greater degree than the control group. Thus, not only were there no differences in headache outcome, but the lowered muscle tension found in the biofeedback group did not affect headache outcome either. This and other studies have called into question the relevance of muscle tension in so-called tension headaches.

Perhaps the most telling study on this topic, however, was carried out by Andrasik and Holroyd.[5] They assigned thirty-nine tension headache sufferers to one of four groups:

1) No treatment;
2) Biofeedback group trained to decrease muscle tension;
3) Biofeedback group trained to increase muscle tension;
4) Biofeedback group trained to achieve a stable level of muscle tension.

All biofeedback groups were given EMG training on the frontalis muscles. All subjects were followed up after six weeks; and some at three years; twenty-eight of the original participants provided headache diary recordings. Results are shown in the diagram shown opposite.

It is clear that *all* the forms of biofeedback showed improvement which was maintained in the long term, but that EMG training to reduce tension was not what caused the improvement. Andrasik and Holroyd argue that the biofeedback training induces psychological changes in the headache sufferers, and that symptom improvement is a result of those changes rather than the specific outcome of muscle tension control. As all treatment groups improved dramatically when compared with the control group, there must be something other than the placebo effect of being hitched up to an electronic device and 'treated' going on, but what is it? All the treatment group subjects successfully obtained changes in muscle tension by conscious control — by

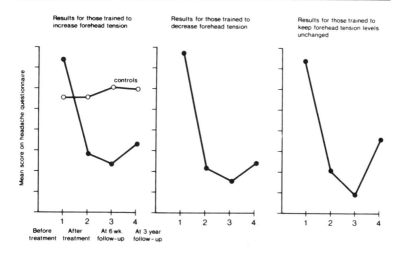

Diagrammatic representation of results redrawn from
Andrasik and Holroyd, showing similarity of outcome in all 3
treatment groups.

focussing their attention on something we do not normally
think about, concentrating on it, and being fed back
information about their success. Is this the key?

Further studies on headache, comparing biofeedback with
relaxation training, and biofeedback with a course of training
in coping strategies in stress situations, have tended to show
that all three types of treatment can be therapeutically
effective with long-term benefits; but biofeedback is not
superior to the other two techniques. The most obvious
common factor in all three treatments is that subjects are
being taught a method of taking control of the problem. They
change from passive pill-takers to managers, which is a
powerful psychological shift.

Biofeedback and Migraine

Biofeedback has not, of course, been used solely in the
treatment of tension headache. Once the principle of
voluntary control of body functions which are usually under
autonomic control was established, the way was open for the
study of many other conditions. Migraine is one example. An
attack of migraine is caused by dilation of blood vessels over
the surface of the brain. As the vessel walls stretch, they

trigger pain-sensitive receptors. The pain is usually severe and usually unilateral in onset. It is characteristically a throbbing pain in the early stages, but may become constant as the attack proceeds. Some forms of migraine are preceded by constriction of the blood vessels, and this early development may result in disturbances of vision. Nausea and vomiting may accompany the other symptoms. Pharmacological treatment is aimed at constricting the blood vessels at the dilation stage, but usually has to be given early on before the vessels become very markedly distended, in order to inhibit the attack.

Biofeedback in the treatment of migraine has involved attempts to increase peripheral blood flow, usually to the hands or fingers. The rationale is that if peripheral blood flow is increased, extra-cranial blood flow will decrease and the affected blood vessels will stop being dilated. (There is no evidence to support this idea; indeed it is unlikely that brain blood flow can be so influenced as there are physiological mechanisms to ensure that blood flow to the vital centres in the brain is maintained within close limits).

However, there is also the argument that increased peripheral blood flow is associated with decreased sympathetic activity in the autonomic nervous system, and therefore with relaxation. Can enhanced peripheral blood flow inhibit migraine? Early investigations often failed to use proper controls and so results were equivocal. Of the many properly controlled studies reviewed by Holmes and Burish[6] none showed biofeedback to be superior to other techniques, such as various methods of relaxation or psychotherapy. In further studies, where subjects were given biofeedback about the pulse amplitude in their temporal arteries, biofeedback was not shown to be superior to other 'treatments'. This suggests that once again the placebo effect accounted for the greatest difference between experimental and control groups.

It is hardly surprising, perhaps, that well-grounded scientific procedures such as biofeedback should fail when they are used in such ways. There is no convincing evidence that anyone can reduce extracranial blood flow by increasing peripheral blood flow, nor that relaxation can be induced by increasing peripheral blood flow (although peripheral blood flow is increased during relaxation, so the *reverse* of the argument is true). Results such as these do not negate the usefulness of biofeedback; they simply demonstrate that it is not some kind of magic that will turn bodily processes topsy-turvy at will. Where it is aimed at a specific response, such as muscular tension or neuromuscular dysfunction, where a causal chain of events is well understood, results are far more impressive and convincing.

Biofeedback and Sphincter Control

N.E. Miller[3] reports on a study designed to retrain patients with organic impairments causing faecal incontinence. They had histories of the problem going back a number of years, but in a few sessions, each of two hours' duration, they learned to respond in such a way as to keep them continent for as long as they were followed up (one and a half to five years). They did this by watching a pen-trace of the responses of their internal and external sphincter muscles to a balloon being inflated and deflated inside the rectum. They were receiving biofeedback which enhanced the pressure change signals from the rectum which precede defaecation. Because of organic impairment they had not been receiving these signals, but biofeedback retrained the response. Although there was no control group in this study, such a highly specific response in a long-term and difficult problem is unlikely to be due to the placebo effect. In this particular condition, it is also unlikely that relaxation training alone would have been useful.

Similar sorts of biofeedback have been used in urinary incontinence. Indeed, the well known bell-and-pad treatment for nocturnal enuresis in children is a biofeedback device. The bell is triggered as soon as the pad is dampened, and this wakes the child who can then get up and finish passing urine in the lavatory. As with the faecal incontinence trainer, the biofeedback enhances a signal which is not being strongly enough received or recognized. Brudny et al[7] have also trained patients with involuntary spasm of the neck muscles on one side (torticollis) to resume the normal position of the head with EMG biofeedback. The patients had long histories and had not responded to various other treatments.

Studies such as these suggest that where there is a well-defined and specific problem, usually involving inadequate signal-detection of neuromuscular changes and where the biofeedback enhances the weak signal, it has indeed a place in therapy. There are many other reported studies demonstrating the success of the technique in retraining muscle function after direct trauma or brain damage, and it seems often to work particularly well as an adjunct to physiotherapy.

Non-specific Changes and Biofeedback

However, where the presenting problem arises from more complex or multi-control systems (such as blood-pressure changes) or where the aetiology is not well established (for example tension headaches or some forms of migraine) then the role of biofeedback as a control-gaining technique is not well established. As we have seen with the headache studies, although biofeedback appears to be doing *something*, its specific action is in question: broader psychological changes involving, perhaps, focussed attention, are postulated as the important underlying change, and these may not need biofeedback at all.

In a study of hypertension in pregnancy, by Little et al,[8] groups treated by relaxation alone, or relaxation with biofeedback, tended to show more improvement than the control group, who were monitored but not treated. Biofeedback did not appear to be superior to relaxation alone. Of the failures in the treated groups, all were nineteen years old or under, and described as 'young unsupported working-class women (who) appeared to be in a high state of anxiety and to have few resources.' The researchers postulated that more intensive counselling with their young 'failures' might have been helpful.

This acknowledges the complex, multifactorial background to hypertension in pregnancy. In a situation such as this, it seems that the non-specific psychological element apparent in the headache studies is operating. There is also the hint that background factors causing high anxiety, such as lack of support, decrease the chances of success in self-control techniques. It would be surprising if this was *not* true; dealing with the emotional and physiological responses to stress while leaving the external causes unchanged can hardly be a recipe for success. This is true, of course, of any self-control technique, not just biofeedback.

In summary, the evidence for the usefulness of biofeedback in conditioning certain neuromuscular responses is well established in the literature. In other studies, it seems that biofeedback and other techniques such as relaxation may operate by effecting psychological changes, but evidence for the *specific* action of biofeedback is wanting. The crucial changes seem to involve focussed attention at the cognitive level, and 'quieting' at the physiological level. It may be that these changes can be effected without using biofeedback in general, although it could be argued that where the learning of attention-focussing and quieting is faulty, biofeedback might aid the learning process by providing additional information about results.

References

1. Miller, N.E. et al, 'Learned modifications of autonomic functions: a review and some new data.' *Circulation Research Supplement*, 1976, 27: 3–11.

2. Shapiro, D. et al, 'Effects of feedback and reinforcement on the control of human systolic blood pressure.' *Science*, 163:588, 1969.

3. Miller, N.E., 'Biofeedback: Evaluation of a new technique.' *New England Journal of Medicine*, March 21 1974, Vol. 290, No. 12, pp. 684–5.

4. Schwartz, G.E., 'Biofeedback, self-regulation and the patterning of physiological processes.' *American Scientist*, May-June 1975, Vol. 63, pp. 314–324.

5. Andrasik, F. and Holroyd, K.A., 'Specific and non-specific effects in the biofeedback treatment of tension headache: 3-year follow-up.' *J. Consulting and Clin. Psychol.*, 1983, Vol. 51, No. 4, pp. 634–636.

6. Holmes, D.S. and Burish,, T.G., 'Effectiveness of biofeedback for treating migraine and tension headaches: a review of the evidence.' *J. Psychosom. Res. 1983*, Vol. 27, No. 6, pp. 515–532.

7. Brudny, J. et. al, 'New therapeutic modality in the treatment of spasmodic torticollis.' *Arch. Phys. Med. Rehabil.*, Vol. 54, p. 575, 1973.

8. Little, B.C. et al, 'Treatment of hypertension in pregnancy by relaxation and biofeedback.' *The Lancet*, 21 April 1984, pp. 865–867.

4. Progressive Muscular Relaxation

It is impossible to say for how far back in history man has understood the value of quietness and rest in illness. At the instinctive level, animals in pain, or sick, or moribund, tend to seek out a quiet and solitary place and to reduce their levels of physical activity to a minimum.

The very earliest institutions devoted to the care of the sick were attached to religious foundations and were therefore places of quiet and peace. In more recent history it was common practice for noise levels to be reduced as much as possible in and around a house where someone lay sick: straw in the streets to muffle the sound of cartwheels, doorknockers wrapped with soft fabric, and household members tiptoeing and whispering, are frequently referred to in accounts from past centuries. In modern times too, hospitals aim for quietness in surroundings, and often restrict visitors by numbers and to certain times of day, while the sick nursed at home are usually kept at lower levels of stimulation and activity than normal. We understand the need to attain a balance between oppressive under-stimulation and over-demanding activity, and while it may be impossible to keep the balance throughout the waking day, the sick, distressed, in pain or dying are habitually given periods of quiet in good care regimes.

In times of acute distress or tension, too, normal background noise levels are often felt as too loud, and there is often the need to seek quietness and solitude for a while. Reducing environmental impact, however, although helpful, is not in itself enough to restore equilibrium to the stressed organism. The search for peace in the external environment may be instinctive, but it needs to be accompanied by certain crucial changes in the body's internal environment if the damaging effects of stress are to be mitigated, pain is to be relieved, or healing facilitated. Quietness or isolation alone may exacerbate the problems of a distressed body and mind; they need to be accompanied by quietness within if they are to work for the good.

In the previous chapter biofeedback has been compared with relaxation training in some of the studies described, and certain common factors have been postulated. Focussed attention and 'quieting' are among them. These involve the changes in thinking, subjective emotional state and physiological arousal, which seem to be important in the management of stress.

Jacobson and After

Modern techniques of relaxation training are based on the pioneering work of Edmund Jacobson in the 1920s and '30s. [1] Jacobson thought that the uncomfortable subjective feeling of anxiety arose largely out of the muscular contractions accompanying increased tension. Therefore relaxation of the muscles would reduce emotional arousal. He showed that blood-pressure and pulse rate, which are raised in emotional states, are reduced by deep muscular relaxation.

Although he occasionally reported using shorter times of treatment, classically Jacobson's subjects were trained to relax forty-four different muscle groups in turn, taking up to an hour to learn to relax each one of the groups. Jacobson did not believe it necessary to add any kind of suggestion to the relaxation training, and did not comment on the sensations subjects might experience. Indeed, he frequently went out of the room between sets of instructions, so that he did not inadvertently influence the subject. In a series of studies, he used EMG recordings to check levels of muscular tension and was able to demonstrate that in untrained subjects tension remains high for a time after muscle contraction, even when the subject is instructed to relax, whereas his trained subjects could abolish the residual tension almost immediately.

Jacobson's technique is long and intensive and requires a high degree of commitment from therapist and client. Although he has acknowledged that certain muscle groups can be combined to speed up the process, he does not recommend the practice. Inherent also in Jacobson's technique is the idea that no further therapeutic assistance will be necessary: once the necessary degree of muscular control has been achieved, people will be able to solve their own emotional problems. He has recommended that people should focus their attention on muscle relaxation at times of emotional stress. Here again is the combination of focussed attention and 'quieting' or relaxation.

Developments of Jacobson's technique are numerous. All subscribe to the same basic idea of progressive muscular relaxation, but most combine muscle groups so that the period of training is shorter. Many modern techniques also seek to aid the sensation of relaxation by contrasting it with tension, so that training may involve first tensing the muscle group, then relaxing. Many also involve the use of suggestions about sensation, which Jacobson completely eschewed. There is no evidence that any of these newer techniques is superior to that proposed by Jacobson. Indeed, Lehrer (1982)[2] argues that the Jacobson technique produces faster,- deeper and longer-lasting levels of muscular relaxation, and he quotes studies to support this view.

The important question is, how crucial is the depth of muscular relaxation in the quieting response? If equally good autonomic quieting and self-control methods for stress relief can be obtained with less deep levels of muscular relxation, in a shorter training time, they should clearly be used in preference to Jacobson's rather cumbersome regime. Jacobson's early work produced strong and long-lasting results with a variety of psychosomatic ailments, including hypertension and asthma, and Lehrer argues that the results are more impressive than those obtained with modern modifications of the technique.

He quotes a study which compared Jacobson's technique with some others and found that Jacobson's produced significant lowering of self-reported anxiety when compared with the others, but changes in measures of physiological arousal, such as heart-rate, were not significantly different between all the groups.

Studies such as these are not easy to evaluate, as Jacobsonian training is so much longer and more intense than others, and that in itself might bias the results. However, it is certainly true that Jacobson has given us an enormously valuable therapeutic tool in relaxation training, and that results from it and its many modified versions continue to help large numbers of people.

Relaxation in the Treatment of Phobic Anxiety

Wolpe (1958)[3] used the induction of relaxation as an integral part of a treatment for phobias, which he called systematic desensitization. Wolpe's technique involves the use of learning procedures to substitute one type of response for another. In desensitization, this means substituting relaxation for anxiety. According to this technique clients describe situations or events which cause them to feel anxious. They are then taught to relax and to imagine the anxiety-provoking situation while remaining relaxed. As anxiety and relaxation are not compatible, the client learns to experience the events in a situation where anxiety is not possible and the theory is that the new response will generalize into the real life situation. Developments of the technique involve clients in producing a hierarchy of anxiety-provoking situations and working through them, beginning with those experienced as mildly anxiety-provoking, and continuing up through the others, building success upon success and creating real-life rather than imagined situations to use with the relaxation response.

Cooke (1966)[4] has compared real-life ('in vivo') and imaginal desensitization of rat phobia, using Jacobson's relaxation training for both groups of subjects, and then exposing them to a hierarchy of anxiety-producing situations involving rats, which one group imagined and the other experienced in real-life. Results showed that both types of desensitization were equally effective, although imaginal procedures are obviously easier to contrive in many situations.

An important point of interest raised by Beech (1969)[5] about studies such as Cooke's, is that the *in vivo* group, although initially trained to relax, could hardly maintain deep levels of muscular relaxation whilst moving about and doing such things as picking up rats. This raises the question of whether the relaxation is a necessary part of the treatment process, as both groups did equally well. It may be that repeated exposure to anxiety-provoking situations, which have previously been avoided, is the crucial factor. Techniques based on repeated exposure without relaxation are known as 'flooding' or 'implosion'. They can be carried out much faster than the little-by-little methods of systematic desensitization pioneered by Wolpe. Results of studies on flooding techniques are mixed. Some success has been reported with certain types of subject, but in the absence of a calming procedure flooding can be an uncomfortably distressing experience, and many subjects prefer desensitization under relaxation. Overall, there is no equivocal evidence of the superiority of flooding over the gentler techniques.

Relaxation clearly has its place as a therapeutic tool in the treatment of phobic anxiety. It acts upon the physiological component of anxiety by facilitating restoration of the steady resting state; it reduces the subjective distress (cognitive component); and it changes the behaviour associated with the phobia by allowing the phobic situation to be faced rather than avoided.

These three aspects of anxiety or arousal are obviously closely inter-related, but they can vary independently to some extent. It is possible for someone to be physiologically calm while experiencing anxious thoughts; to be physiologically aroused, but with a blank mind; or to be physiologically and cognitively calm, but continue to carry out an old pattern of behaviour based on anxiety. To quote one example: in a case of phobic anxiety about being in an enclosed space, for some time after the subjective feeling of anxiety and the phobic behaviour was abolished, episodes of sudden physiological arousal occurred for no obvious reason. These episodes were finally controlled with relaxation training, but they were the last component of a raised level of anxiety to go away. Cases such as this highlight the fact that, not withstanding Jacobson's earlier claims, relaxation training of the muscles alone is unlikely to be as effective as using relaxation to facilitate control of *all* the components of anxiety as Wolpe did.

Problems in Research
The method to be used in relaxation training is even now a matter of debate. Hillenberg and Collins (1982)[6] have carried out a procedural analysis and review of relaxation training research from 1970 to 1979. Among the target problems investigated are sleep disturbance, headache, hypertension, examination anxiety, general anxiety, speech anxiety, asthma,

drinking behaviour, hyperactivity, and anger control. They report that relaxation training is 'typically effective' as a therapeutic technique in accounts from the literature. However, in the eighty studies reviewed there was found wide variability in types of relaxation procedure used, number of relaxation training sessions, the use of live or taped instructions, and the use of home practice instructions. Some researchers failed to specify what they did. This makes comparison between studies impossible, and only broad generalizations can be made.

Relaxation training obviously is a widely used and successful therapeutic tool, but its precise methodology, range and limits of use have not yet been established. Hillenberg and Collins have made a plea for standardized procedures to be used in scientific studies of relaxation so that it can be properly evaluated. In the meantime a variety of techniques called relaxation training, all of which are rooted in Jacobson's work but which have branched out individually, continue to be used.

The techniques have in common the use of muscular relaxation as a means of facilitating physiological 'quieting'. In other words, they represent a method of controlling or conditioning some of the activity of the autonomic nervous system. During relaxation, the physiological stress response is inhibited, and studies have shown that regular practice of relaxation over a period of four to six weeks can lower the resting pulse rate and stabilize other components of autonomic arousal, such as cardiac output and blood-pressure. These changes gradually extend beyond the period of relaxation and can become relatively stable features of daily life. This is a learning process, and it is obvious that it will be affected by the care with which it is taught and carried out. The use of audiotaped instructions will probably have some effect; occasional practice will have some effect. Learning will be facilitated, however, where the technique is properly explained and taught, and followed up by a supervised regime of home practice. Taped instructions are then very useful. As the optimum amount of practice has not been established scientifically, it is perhaps best to regard progressive relaxation as a skill, like playing a musical instrument, where smooth gains are made by the use of a regular regime of daily practice.

Make the most of relaxation — it should be enjoyable.

A Relaxation Regime

A typical set of instructions might begin by explaining to the would-be progressive relaxer that a quiet and comfortable ambience is important. The room should be reasonably warm but airy, without strong light. A bed is the best place to relax on, but a sofa, or the floor with cushions, or a comfortable armchair can be used. Shoes and tight clothing should be removed.

Some sets of instructions, like Jacobson's, concentrate on relaxing each muscle group. Others begin by tensing each muscle group and encouraging the practising relaxer to experience that sensation first, and then to relax and feel the contrast. Relaxing from a state of tension is a more vivid experience. This is a specimen set of instructions:

First of all, screw the toes up. Do this in a slow and controlled manner, without snatching at the muscles. Let the tension build up slowly, hold it briefly, then let all that tension go, and relax.

Next move the toes the other way; pull them up towards your head. Don't move the rest of your feet or legs. Once again, let the tension build up slowly, hold it, then relax and feel all the tightness flow away.

Now tighten the calf muscles by stretching your legs away from you. Make your legs feel half an inch longer. Hold it; now relax again and rest.

Now push your knees together. Keep pushing and you will feel the big muscles in your thighs begin to tighten up. Hold it; then relax and let all the tension flow away.

Now tighten the muscles in your bottom. Pull them in, hold it, and relax.

Now the muscles in your abdomen. First push out, and make your abdomen as round and firm as you can. Hold it, then relax. Now pull the muscles in, and make yourself as flat as you can. Hold it, and relax.

Now tense and then relax the muscles in your back. Keeping your bottom and shoulders on the bed, arch up the middle of your back. Do this gently, but feel the pull on the muscles, and then let yourself relax again.

Now we'll start with your hands. As with the toes, first screw your fingers into a fist, really tight. Then relax. Now pull your fingers back the other way, towards your shoulders. Pull, and then relax. Now stretch your hands and arms out away from you. Feel the pull, feel the tension, right up to your shoulders. Then relax. Just let your arms flop gently back on to the bed.

Now that your arms and legs and lower trunk are relaxed, let's think about your breathing. It isn't necessary to breathe extra deeply when you want to relax, in fact, it isn't a good idea as it can make you feel unwell if you overdo it, but it is a good idea to get a nice, steady, controlled rhythm of breathing going, to aid relaxation.

One way to do this is to count as you breathe — in, two, three, hold, out, two, three. Keep on breathing easily and steadily to the count of three. Breathe in a sense of calm and peace, and each time you breathe out, let go and relax a little more. Calm on the in-breath and relax on the out-breath. Take ten to fifteen breaths in this steady easy fashion.

Now we'll go on to your shoulders, neck and head. First pull your shoulderblades together. Remember to move in a steady and controlled way. Hold it and relax again. Next, shrug. Pull your shoulders up towards your ears, feel the tension, relax.

Now turn your head to one side, and feel the tension in the other side of your neck. Then relax. Now the other side, and then relax. Now push your head back, as if you were trying to burrow a hole in the pillow. Then relax.

Now the muscles in your forehead and scalp. First push your eyebrows up, as if you were trying to look extremely surprised. Now relax and let all that tension smooth away. Now frown hard, and pull all the muscles the other way. Then relax.

Now close your eyes and screw them up tight. Hold it, then relax. Keep your eyes closed if you want to — do whatever feels comfortable.

Now lift your tongue up to the roof of your mouth and push. Hold it, then relax.

Now push your bottom teeth in front of your top teeth. Push, then relax.

Now you should be feeling relaxed and heavy, and content to stay where you are for a while.

Cognitive Quieting

Physical relaxation takes only a few minutes. It focusses the attention and has a quieting effect on the body. In many people it is in itself relaxing enough to induce sleep. However, the possibility that subjective feelings of anxiety will remain, even when bodily relaxation is accomplished, should also be dealt with. To this end, a further period of instruction, involving relaxing mental imagery, may be used, with or without music as an additional aid. The person relaxing may use free imagination if it can be controlled so as to promote relaxation. Alternatively, the scene may be set by the therapist. Here is one example:

Imagine that you have been walking through a wood and have come to the shore of a lake. It is a summer evening, and the light is soft. By the lake is a big old tree with mossy roots. It looks comfortable. Sit down amongst the roots and lean against the trunk. It *is* comfortable; rather like sitting in an armchair. Rest your back against the trunk and look out over the lake. Notice how large an expanse of water it is. You can just see distant shapes on the horizon; you are just aware of rocks and trees around the edges; but most of what you can see is water. Notice how still it is. The air is moving a little, stirring the water gently, moving the leaves on the trees gently. You can hear the soft noise of the leaves rustling, and the lap, lap of the water touching the shore, but otherwise all is quiet. Go on looking out across the lake.

When you have been looking across the still water for a while, you notice something. Floating out on the middle of the lake is an old-fashioned wooden cart-wheel, just floating on the surface of the water. Your attention is drawn to it. Go on looking at it. As you look you notice that as the wheel is floating it is also beginning to turn. Very slowly, almost imperceptibly, it is turning round. It is turning so slowly that unless you watch it all the time, you would miss the fact that it is moving at all. Go on watching the wheel, floating and turning. Now you begin to notice something else. As the wheel is turning round, it is also beginning to sink. Very slowly, turning and sinking. Turning and sinking slowly into the cool, still water. You can breathe under the water like a fish or a mermaid. Let yourself sink into the calm water. You can float down to the bottom and sleep. If you sleep, you will sleep as long as you want to or need to, and wake feeling refreshed and calm. Or you can stay drifting, floating between sleeping and waking, relaxed and calm, for as long as you want.

When you have finished relaxing, move your arms and legs around a little, and let yourself float up towards the surface and break through. Open your eyes. When you want to sit up, do so slowly, swinging your feet down first and bringing your head up last, to give yourself time to adapt.

There are many variations on this technique. Some therapists prefer to instruct on one leg at a time, then one arm, to enhance the feeling of contrast. Some do not use tension at first, but go straight into relaxation. Yet others do not use muscle groups, but instruct whole body relaxation. The use of mental imagery is also a matter of choice, although it is certainly useful in dealing with anxious thoughts and subjective feelings.

The physical exercises described for progressive muscular relaxation should be carried out in a controlled and gentle way, and should not hurt. For the great majority of people they are easy to manage and present no problems. However, for some people, for example those with fibrositic pain, arthritis, or any conditions where muscle movement, no matter how gentle, can be painful, an alternative method might be more suitable. One such is autogenic training.

Autogenic Training

A technique developed in the early years of the century by hypnotherapists Vogt and Schultz is known as autogenic training. They were working in sleep and hypnosis research and noticed that people who could put themselves into a hypnotic state (i.e. autogenic) also reported that they were learning to control stress and fatigue, and to eliminate stress-related headaches and other symptoms, by using the technique. The work has been more lately developed by Luthe[7] (from 1960 onwards) and is now a standard method of stress control.

A recent report by Medik and Fursland[8] describes classes in the technique at a health centre. Patients undergoing the training had been referred for a variety of problems including phobias, migraine, insomnia, 'nervous stomach' and high blood-pressure. Eighty-two per cent found the classes generally helpful and seventy-four per cent found that they helped specific symptoms too. Most of those who attended also reported feeling more relaxed and confident. As with other relaxation techniques, regular practice over a period of weeks produced results. The study was not well-controlled, so the benefits obtained cannot be ascribed to the autogenic method (rather than a placebo effect) beyond the shadow of a doubt, but the results are encouraging and merit further investigation.

Autogenic training begins with adopting a relaxed posture, on a chair, or on a bed. (Two other positions are sometimes used: one is sitting on the floor, spine relaxed, head forward on a hard stool; one is sitting on a chair with arms across thighs, head forward. Both are likely to cause discomfort or backache and should probably be avoided.) Then one concentrates on breathing in feelings of relaxation, and breathing out tension and pain. The attention may then be focussed on any tense or painful parts of the body. No attempt is made to change anything: the mind is merely allowed to dwell on that part, and to explore it uncritically.

Next, the physical sensations of the hypnotic state are re-created. These are basically warmth and heaviness, and are achieved by concentrating on 'trigger' phrases or formulae, as follows, which are repeated silently, with pauses in between:

My right arm is heavy;
My left arm is heavy;
My right arm is warm;
My left arm is warm;
My right leg is heavy;
My left leg is heavy;
My left leg is warm;
My right leg is warm;
My heartbeat is calm and regular;
My breathing is calm and regular;
My forehead is cool and light;
I am at peace with myself and fully relaxed.

At each phrase, participants 'find' that part of the body and concentrate on it passively. No effort is made to accomplish the desired change, it is a process of letting go.

A recent study used 100 healthy men and women aged between twenty-five and sixty who were tested on a number of psychological and physical measures designed to pick out stress-related variables and heart disease risk factors. Then half the group undertook a two-month physical training course, and half, autogenic training. At the end of the study, both groups experienced reductions in anxiety and depression and improved their scores on general health questionnaires. Both groups reported an enhanced sense of well-being, improved sleep pattern, and decrease of physical tension. Both groups showed significant reductions in resting pulse rate, blood-pressure and blood fatty acids. The important point here is that relaxation and passive concentration can be health-enhancing, and that these techniques are open to all. Jogging, aerobics, working-out, all these physically active methods can be very good at improving health, but they are obviously not suitable for everyone. They exclude a wide range of people who are not fully physically fit, and moreover, should not be embarked upon by many people with high heart-disease risk factors, without a slow build-up under medical supervision. Autogenic training, on the other hand, can be practised by anyone — on top of a bus, in a wheelchair or in a hospital bed.

Relaxation in Therapy

The fundamental tools of relaxation or autogenic training may need to be used in a formal therapeutic context. Any quieting technique is unlikely to be harmful to most people, and there is nothing to stop anyone using a self-taught technique at home. However, assistance with learning the technique initially, and checking that it is right, can be invaluable. In addition, most problems involving stress or anxiety have a behavioural component, and that too may need active intervention, as it can be hard to accomplish change alone. Taking control of the problem and effecting change might need some sort of outside help in the initial stages, perhaps from a counsellor, or a doctor or psychologist, or in a group or workshop on stress management.

Such workshops are gradually becoming more common. For example, Barry Hopson and his colleagues at the Counselling and Career Development Unit at the University of Leeds have developed training programmes and workshops to help people cope with the 'transitional' stresses typified by the Holmes and Rahé Social Readjustment Scale (see page 40). As part of the initial programme, participants are asked to fill in a questionnaire on coping skills. It helps them to identify areas in which they need help to develop appropriate skills and behaviour. In the workshops, people help each other to develop and practise the crucial skills.

The questions cover areas like knowing yourself and the situation you are in, knowing people who can help, learning from similar past experiences, knowing how to look after yourself (including knowing how to relax), letting go of the past, making plans of action, and looking for the gains one has made. Working with other people in learning situations can transform stress from a potentially destructive force into a vehicle for personal growth and gain in a one-to-one situation. A typical therapeutic strategy aimed at taking control of the problem and effecting change might be as follows:

1) The client produces, usually verbally, but sometimes in writing, as detailed an account as possible of the problem (s), including the onset and progression, the situations in which it occurs, the thoughts, feelings and physical sensations accompanying it, how it affects behaviour at all levels — from sleep and appetite to social intercourse.

2) The therapist and client work out a list of priorities of

aspects of the problem to be addressed. It is often the case that the major focus of the problem, which might be an inability to eat in public for the fear of choking, for example, or a lifestyle severely curtailed by tension headaches or stress-related high blood-pressure, is hemmed in by other, apparently less significant troubles which must be dealt with first. Such things as a disturbed pattern of sleeping, or habitually rushed eating habits, or over-attention to the details of housework so that no time is left in the day for rest or recreation, often accompany a central problem. Helping a client to re-think and reorganize parts of the day so as to change one or two pieces of maladaptive behaviour introduces and underlines the notion of self-management, which is a crucial factor in therapeutic change.

The next step might be to teach the client a relaxation technique, giving a sound rationale for its use. An air of mystique left about it might enhance the placebo effect in the short term, but is not conducive to self-management strategies. Identifying with precision the problems resulting in the ill health or disease and changing what can be changed, including the maladaptive physiological response to stress, are the fundamental aspects of the attack on stress-related conditions. Relaxation techniques have proved to be simple but effective equipment in helping people to overcome such things as phobic anxiety, headache, other pain related to tension, high blood-pressure, some gastric disorders, insomnia, and various sorts of anxiety and maladaptive emotional response. It has been shown that relaxation can protect certain types of people from recurrent heart attacks by helping them to attain periods of physiological quieting and to change an over-stressed lifestyle.

Schwartz et al [9] report a case of a woman who presented herself at the emergency room of the local hospital up to twenty times a month, following a mild heart attack from which she had made an excellent physical recovery. Her chest pain, which was the reason for her trips to hospital, was felt to be primarily muscular, and to be both triggered and amplified by excessive anxiety accompanied by hyperventilation (over-breathing) and obsessive fear of a further heart attack. She was treated by educative counselling about the nature of this pain, and by learning to control her muscle tension and breathing with relaxation, assisted by biofeedback. Her family were also helped not to reinforce her behaviour, whereas previously they had joined in the panic, taking her to hospital each time she had chest pain. Treatment was once a week for two months. During the first week she visited the emergency room ten times. By the eighth week she had three weeks free of any such visits, and she reported significant increases in her social life activities, shopping and exercise tolerance. She was by then using relaxation as required, that is, when she felt an increase in tension. At eight months follow-up, no emergency room visits were recorded. Chest pain still sometimes occurred in response to stress, but was dealt with by relaxation.

Relaxation and Pain
Relaxation training as a means of changing the response to pain is increasingly used in pain-control clinics. It is perhaps at its most effective when the onset of pain is accompanied by a sudden and dramatic increase in anxiety level and increased muscle tension. Most forms of severe pain are associated with increased muscular tone, which may be confined to an area immediately around the primary pain, or more generalised, or at a site far distant from the source. Clenching the jaw, for example, may accompany abdominal pain; low back pain often involves an increase in tension of back, buttock and leg muscles; some chest and abdominal pain results in increased muscle tone all over the body. Whilst the primitive function of the increased tone might be to 'guard' the primary pain site and prevent damaging movement, it is not useful in pain which is not associated with acute inflammation or injury. Indeed, in non-acute pain the increased muscle tension often causes secondary pain and thus exacerbates the original problem. Severe pain is also accompanied by subjective feelings of distress, and physiological arousal. All these things — the increased muscle tone, the arousal and the distress — can be brought under control by successful relaxation training.

In the case reported by Schwartz et al, the relaxation inhibited the pain, and prevented the onset of panic and the unnecessary trip to the emergency room. Several studies of asthma with an identifiable stress component in the onset have also been described. As with pain, the first intimation of breathing difficulties is accompanied by a sudden excess of subjective anxiety and autonomic arousal. This can exacerbate the problem, as extreme anxiety often results in a panting kind of breathing pattern, and a feeling of tight-chestedness. Relaxation with particular emphasis on breath control can inhibit such attacks. In stress-induced asthma and in chronic pain, the individual's whole perspective on the problem is changed once they can control the panic associated with onset. When the panic has been inhibited, the sense of being in an out-of-control situation goes too, and management of the incident becomes possible.

In another example, a thirty-year-old housewife had developed severe tension headaches after the birth of her child. The pain was incapacitating and was associated with an upsurge of anxiety, as she felt that her care of the child and the house, and her relationship with her husband, were adversely affected by the frequent attacks, during which she could do nothing but lie on the sofa, cradling her head in her arms.

It was an uphill struggle for this woman to accept that the pain was stress-related and could be controlled by relaxation training, and for some weeks she resisted trying it. However, relations with her husband had begun to deteriorate and that eventually gave her the impetus to try to learn the technique. As she became skilled at relaxing, and the pains became less frequent and less severe, she was encouraged to look at her lifestyle and consider the stresses inherent in it. For example, she was overly house-proud and devoted much time and energy to keeping the house always clean and tidy. The baby's health, which was excellent, was also a source of enormous anxiety, and her fears were bound up with dirt and germs there too. On most days she had failed to meet her own impossible standards, and was exhausted and upset by the time her husband came in from work. Once her pain was controlled, and she was able to take a calmer look at her situation, she was able to order her priorities more realistically: she accepted that the house was first and foremost a home, and not a showplace, and that she could enjoy the baby so much more when he was allowed to romp around and get a little grubby and not treated like a precious doll. Over the course of six months she learned to keep herself pain-free much of the time, and to keep her anxiety level down to a reasonable level too.

Relaxation and High Blood-pressure

High blood-pressure is another problem which has been successfully treated with relaxation training. Agras et al [10] treated thirty patients with essential hypertension. All had diastolic blood-pressures greater than 90mm Hg (see footnote on page 50), and were randomly assigned to relaxation training or blood-pressure monitoring (as a control). The initial relaxation or monitoring programme took place over an eight-week period, and participants were followed up fifteen months later. Blood-pressure recordings were taken in the clinic, and at intervals during the normal working day, using an ambulatory blood-pressure monitor which provided twenty-four measurements at twenty-minute intervals.

It was reported that both in the clinic and during the working day the relaxation training group shared significant lowering of the diastolic blood-pressure when compared with the control group. In the period between initial treatment and follow-up, all subjects had received bi-monthly boosters of relaxation training, or measurement only, depending on their group. Studies such as this suggest that an intensive period of initial training and intermittent 'booster' sessions can provide a means of control of high blood-pressure which persists over time.

The role of post-treatment practice was looked at by Libo and Arnold.[11] They studied fifty-eight patients who had undergone relaxation training with biofeedback for a variety of conditions, including migraine, tension headache, mixed headache, chronic pain, anxiety and essential hypertension. Patients were followed up from one to five years after therapy and in all diagnostic groups, of those who had continued to practise relaxation, eighty-six per cent had improved, while only five per cent of those who had stopped practising had improved. Patients who were practising only occasionally, as needed, or when stressed, improved as much or more than those who practised regularly and frequently. This result underlines the importance of self-awareness and self-management in the control of stress-related conditions. The most significant improvers were those who monitored their needs and practised when they knew they needed to, rather than following a set regime.

Another study, which used a variety of diagnostic groups in a programme involving an eight-week initial training, and follow-up at three, six, twelve and twenty-four months (Ford et al [12]) showed that unsuccessful (unimproved) patients tended to show elevated levels of psychological stress through the follow-up period. Again, this shows that relaxation training alone has no magic power to improve health if background stressors remain at a high level. It needs to be part of an integrated and well-considered change of behaviour in order to be truly effective. Physiological quieting and cognitive calm also provide thinking time. Quieting, cognitive calming and positive behavioural change constitute the corner stones of long-lasting and effective stress management.

While results from the scientific literature give no clear guide as to the most effective method of relaxation, or the precise use of it for maximum effect, there are indications that a variety of relaxation techniques have been found to be useful; even an eight-week training course of simple relaxation, with booster follow-up, can help lower and stabilize high blood-pressure. However, the deliberate use of relaxation to counteract stress when it occurs is one step further along the road to stress management, and the ultimate success seems to come when the physiological, cognitive and behavioural components of the stress response are all taken under conscious control.

References

1. Jacobson, E., *Progressive Relaxation* (University of Chicago Press, 1938).
2. Lehrer, P.M., 'How to relax and how not to relax: a re-evaluation of the work of Edmund Jacobson.' *J. Behav. Res. Ther.* Vol. 20, pp. 417–428, 1982.
3. Wolpe J., *Psychotherapy by Reciprocal Inhibition* (Stanford University Press, 1958).
4. Cooke, G., 'The efficacy of two desensitization procedures: an analogue study.' *J. Behav. Res. Ther.* Vol. 4, pp. 17–24, 1966.
5. Beech, H.R., *Changing Man's Behaviour* (Penguin, 1969).
6. Hillenberg, J.B. and Collins, F.L.J., 'A procedural analysis and review of relaxation training research.' *J. Behav. Res. Ther.* Vol. 20, pp. 251–260, 1982.

7. Luthe, W. and Schultz, J., *Autogenic Therapy* (Grune and Stratton Inc., New York, 1969).

8. Medik, L. and Fursland, A., 'Maximising scarce resources: Autogenic relaxation classes at a health centre.' *British Journal of Medical Psychology.* Vol 57, pp. 181–185, 1984.

9. Schwartz, D.P. et al, 'A chronic emergency room visitor with chest pain: successful treatment by stress management training and biofeedback.' *Pain,* 18 (1984) pp. 315–319.

10. Agras, W.S. et al, 'Long term persistence of relaxation induced blood-pressure lowering during the working day.' *J. Consult. and Clin. Psychol.,* 1983, Vol. 51, No. 5, pp. 792–794.

11. Libo, L.M. and Arnold, G.E., 'Relaxation practice after biofeedback therapy: a long term follow-up study of utilization and effectiveness.' *Biofeedback and Self-Regulation,* Vol. 8, No. 2, 1983.

12. Ford, M.R. et al, 'Quieting response training: predictors of long-term outcome.' *Biofeedback and Self-Regulation,* Vol. 8, No. 3, 1983.

5. Eastern Influences

Quietness

The value of relaxation in modifying the body's response to stress has been well established. Jacobson's work pioneered the use of progressive muscular relaxation as a formalized therapeutic technique. He used it successfully as a treatment for a variety of stress-related disorders, including psychosomatic problems. His work, and that of many who came after him, has demonstrated that in most people deep muscular relaxation is accompanied by physiological 'quieting' and subjective feelings of calmness and well-being. Wolpe showed how these two aspects of stress-reduction could be used in desensitization programmes to modify behaviour, too. Thus the subjective (cognitive), somatic (physiological) and behavioural aspects of the stress response can be changed by this relatively simple technique.

It has, however, been argued that there are individual differences in the way that these components of anxiety are expressed. In some people the physical sensations predominate. When people tend to experience anxiety as 'butterflies in the stomach', i.e. shaking, sweating, breathing difficulties and so on, they have been described as 'somatically anxious'.[1] When the predominant pattern associated with anxiety is a flood of distressing thoughts or unpleasant subjective feelings, the sufferers are called 'cognitively anxious'. Not everyone is inevitably one or the other type, and many of us feel both cognitive and somatic distress when we are anxious. However, Norton and Johnson have argued that where there is a predominant trend in someone, different techniques of stress-reduction may be required. Quieting techniques with the accent on physical relaxation may succeed better with the somatically anxious, whereas those who are cognitively anxious might be better suited with a more mentalistic approach (i.e. one using imagination).

Where deep physical relaxation can be achieved, but is still accompanied by feelings of distress, an imaginal technique (such as the one described on page 68) can be helpful. Sometimes, in cases such as this, biofeedback is used with relaxation, as having to focus the attention on the biofeedback device can help to calm the mind. There is also a range of techniques under the generic heading of 'meditation', where the main emphasis is on cognitive quieting. Some of these techniques involve the use of exercises or specific movements or postures (such as T'ai Ch'i and some forms of Yoga) and some do not, but the emphasis is on changing thoughts and feelings.

Meditation

Just as the need for quietness in sickness and distress goes far back into the history of humankind, the use of meditation as a means of achieving a deep sense of calm, and often a heightened inner awareness, is part of our earliest recorded past. The use of meditation in the religious life was part of Buddha's teaching, and it comes all the way through history to modern Buddhists and other religious groups, including some Christian sects.

Techniques of meditation have been, and still are, used as a means of attaining an altered state of consciousness which has special qualities and which may be described as attaining Nirvana, cosmic awareness, the still deep centre of the self, reaching God. Whatever the spiritual purpose of meditation, it produces a deep and satisfying sense of well-being in those who practise it successfully. As with relaxation training, the feeling tends to extend beyond the time spent in practising the technique, into daily life, after a time. Many of those who practise different types of meditation attribute enhanced physical good health to its regular use, as well as intellectual and emotional gains in strength and efficiency, and deepening spiritual awareness. It can be that while such beliefs can be off-putting for some people, many others find them an extra source of strength and comfort.

Many techniques of meditation originate in the East, and

although there they may have histories stretching back before written records, they have tended to have a more recent impact in the West. Ever since occidental man journeyed to the orient, some individuals have returned fascinated by aspects of the different cultures and have tried such things as Yoga or Zen. However, it is only in the latter half of this century that these practices have become more widespread and available here.

Yoga

Yoga is a good example of the Eastern influence on the West. It is sometimes thought of nowadays as just a method of keeping fit, but it is much more than that. Yoga is an ancient art or discipline whose ultimate aim is union with the Divine or Infinite. It has physical and meditative aspects. Although its method was first committed to writing in around 200 B.C. by a guru (teacher) named Patanjali, he was recording an oral tradition that went back for generations and the origins of which are lost in ancient history.

There are several forms of Yoga, but the one most commonly practised in the West is Hatha Yoga, or physical Yoga. It is a form of training aimed at bodily and mental fitness and control. The body is made fit by the use of a series of postures or *asanas*, which are carried out regularly. These postures are meant to massage the internal organs and thus promote fitness. However, simple physical fitness is only part of it. The student of Yoga is also expected to follow a code of ethics or conduct, as follows:

— the aspiring Yogi should not destroy or injure anything;
— should be truthful;
— should not steal;
— should not covet other people's possessions;
— should practise self-control and be moderate in the use of food, drink and sex;
— should keep inwardly and outwardly clean;
— should be contented;
— should practise self-discipline, tolerance, patience and mental calmness;
— should educate him- or herself;
— should try to surrender the mind and self to a higher power, while sharing the good fortune with others.

Notice that control and a quiet and contented mind, feature strongly in this list. There are also instructions about the regulation of the bowels, about diet, and about relaxation — and there is much more to Yoga than this. (There are several good books with basic information for those who want to read further.) The strict mental and physical discipline required of serious students of Yoga and other Eastern philosophies does not suit us all.

. . . just keeps on saying 'aum'.

However, the basic ideas of a healthy body and a quiet mind are obviously sound and within reach of many. Choosing a method of achieving them which is suitable to your personality and circumstance is the key to success. Most people find that the regular practice of physical Yoga enhances feelings of good health and well-being, and is a calming influence on the mind. This is all possible with the regular exercise routine, which may be used beneficially without the adoption of the whole philosophy.

T'ai Ch'i

Yoga, although a relatively gentle form of exercise, is sometimes found to be too strenuous by some people. Another example of a healthful and relaxing form of exercise, based on a series of gentle, circular, rhythmic movements, and suitable for most people, including those of an advanced age, is T'ai Ch'i or T'ai Ch'i Chuan. It is based on an ancient Chinese philosophy concerned with balancing various forces in the body, and promoting the flow *chi* (energy, life-force).

Like Yoga, T'ai Ch'i is a very old discipline. It was founded in the Sung dynasty by a Taoist named Chang San-feng, for health and self-defence. The movements are slow and beautiful, like a classical dance. Unlike Yoga, the movements flow continuously; there is no holding of postures.

YANG– heat, motion
outward centrifugal force

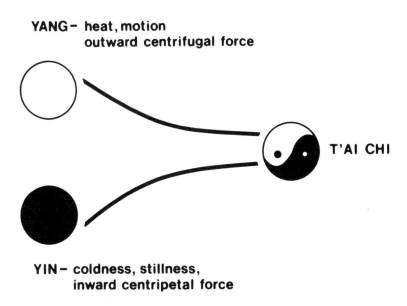

T'AI CHI

YIN– coldness, stillness,
inward centripetal force

The balancing of forces in T'ai Ch'i.

To quote from a modern T'ai Ch'i master, T.T. Liang, writing in 1977,

'I am nearing eighty years old and have been practising T'ai Ch'i for more than thirty years... in the beginning I took up T'ai Ch'i in order to save my life after a grave illness ... . I gradually became more interested in trying to make the art both more scientific and aesthetic. I introduced rhythm so that postures can be practised to music, slowly, effortlessly and continuously. After sufficient practice you will master the 150 postures so thoroughly that you will forget the rhythm, the movement, even yourself... this is meditation in action, and action in meditation... this is complete relaxation of mind and body.

T.T. Liang says that, when you have mastered the art, a daily practice of thirty minutes takes you out of this world so full of tension, noise, politics and danger, into an ideal world of peacefulness and quiet. Again, the central emphasis is on a regular daily period of bodily relaxation and mental concentration, as in all the techniques, old and new, so far described.

Most forms of meditation have some rituals, or religious or quasi-religious beliefs associated with the practice, which are thought to be essential to the success of the meditation.

Transcendental Meditation

There are numerous other variations on the basic idea of using some sort of mental device to achieve the desired state. One technique of meditation with an almost world-wide following has received much publicity since the broadening of its use outside India, where it was first developed. Transcendental meditation, or TM, is estimated to have more than a million devotees in most countries of the world, outside Russia and China. The TM movement was founded by the Maharishi Mahesh Yogi who was himself for many years a pupil of Guru Dev, a spiritual teacher in a remote part of the Himalayas.

In 1955 the Maharishi left the Himalayas and travelled around India, teaching. Many people, particularly the young, were drawn by his teaching, and in 1957 he established the Spiritual Regeneration Movement in Madras, southern India. He then began to travel around outside India — to Singapore, Hawaii, California, New York and Europe. So many people wanted to learn TM by then that it was clear that he could not teach them all himself, and he therefore began to train teachers, at first in Rishikesh, in Northern India, and then in Europe as the ever-increasing demand grew. Now, as well as the training institutes, there is the Maharishi International University which integrates TM with conventional academic disciplines, and the Foundation for the Science of Creative Intelligence, the primary concern of which is to introduce the benefits of TM to business and industry.

In the thirty years since the technique began to reach a wider public, interest in it has grown at an amazingly rapid rate and there are numerous claims for its positive benefits on a personal and social level. Maharishi chose the term 'transcendental' (going beyond) to indicate that TM takes its practitioners beyond the usual level of wakefulness to a state of profound rest coupled with a heightened awareness. It is believed to be a powerful method of stress-reduction as well as a means of opening or sensitizing the mind to a new level of awareness, so that personal functioning is enhanced.

The mantra

In TM the body is at rest, and attention is turned from the complex and busy surface levels of the mind to its quieter depths. This is achieved by the inner repetition of a mantra. Mantras are Sanskrit words which have no denotative meaning and which therefore should be free of distracting associations. Attention is focussed on them as sound-patterns, and is thereby disengaged from other concerns. The sound-patterns they make are believed to produce soothing and harmonious vibrations in the mind which aid the quieting process.

TM directs the attention inwards and downwards, to where thought is considered to arise in a pure and simple state. Thought floats up from these quiet and unelaborated depths to the (conscious) surface. In the quiet depths of the mind thought has a special quality. The mind is deeply still and calm, and yet in a state of heightened awareness. This is the 'going beyond' state, which transcends our visual level of wakeful awareness. The vehicle for this re-direction of thought is the mantra.

The mantra is given to a pupil meditator by his teacher during the first individual teaching session. The session begins with a short ceremony, which is not meant to be religious (although in essence it is a sort of religious ritual) where an offering of fruit and flowers, brought by the pupil, is made.

Before the pupil and teacher meet in private, the would-be pupil will have attended two public lectures, during which the nature of TM and the benefits of its practice are explained. Those who wish to go on to learn TM need to commit themselves to the further personal instruction session and follow-up meetings on three successive days after that. There is then a further 'checking' session. Pupils are also asked to abstain from non-prescribed drugs for 15 days prior to instruction, so that the meditation is not interfered with, and also to pay a fee. Thus there is a required commitment of time, effort, and money, and the need to forego the habitual psychological props provided by non-prescribed drugs. All these things are important: they help to ensure that no-one undertakes the programme lightly and without a great deal of thought. No programme of positive life-change is likely to succeed without commitment.

Transcendental Meditation and Change

Numerous claims about the power of TM as an instrument of positive change have been made. Unique physiological, emotional, intellectual and social gains are reported, and many studies have been carried out to investigate those reports. From a scientific point of view many of the studies are disappointing, as they are poorly controlled. The placebo effect mentioned earlier can bedevil any technique aimed at therapeutic change, and this includes TM. Any claims made for its effectiveness must be substantiated by:

a) showing the effect to be greater than placebo;
b) showing the effect to be a unique property of TM itself, and not something else.

For example, it can be shown that during TM oxygen consumption and carbon dioxide elimination are reduced, as the rate of breathing decreases. However, the same response can be obtained from other activities involving quiet surroundings, sitting or lying comfortably, relaxing, and using a mental (cognitive) device for focussing thoughts. Thus, the change in breathing pattern is a property of many relaxation techniques, and is not unique to one. It is enhanced, not by any particular technique, but by increasing practice and skill with the chosen method.

Several studies have compared these and other physiological changes which are related to autonomic quieting, using experienced TM practitioners to compare with people using other techniques. Not surprisingly, TM apparently shows greater effects. It is like comparing the levels of muscular relaxation attained by experienced Jacobson-type relaxers with those of novices using shorter methods. Quieting skills go on improving with practice; no new learner will attain levels comparable to those reached by the experts. In order to establish whether meditation is unique in its physiological effects, advanced practitioners would have to be compared with those equally experienced in other self-regulatory techniques.

In several studies reviewed by D.H. Shapiro[2] such things as changes in blood-pressure, respiration and pulse rate were found to be common to a variety of relaxing strategies, such as TM, progressive relaxation and other instructional relaxation techniques. Just sitting quietly and listening to music can produce, in some people, physiological quieting responses comparable to those obtained during TM, when both groups are particularly tense to start with. Thus, the magnitude of the changes recorded in relaxation studies depends on the initial level of tension, as well as the successful use of any particular technique.

Transcendental Meditation and Electroencephalographs

Some claims have been made for a pattern of brain waves unique to TM, which are thought to reflect the 'alert-yet-deeply-resting' paradox of the successful TM state. It has also been suggested that the emotional and reasoning parts of the brain, which can often be at odds, work together in synchrony during TM. In most people, the analytical, reasoning functions of the brain are represented in the left cerebral hemisphere, and the more intuitive, emotional kind of thinking in the right cerebral hemisphere.

Some studies on TM have claimed that electroencephalographic (EEG) recordings show evidence of synchrony between the two hemispheres during meditation. It is argued that creative intelligence requires the synthesis of both analytic and intuitive thinking, and that the EEG studies show that TM facilitates this.

Unfortunately, the synchronicity has not been demonstrated in some studies. In other pieces of research, periods of synchronicity have been shown to occur in TM and other relaxation techniques, but the meaning of such variations in EEG is not known. It is an interesting idea that such brain-wave patterns mean that creative intelligence is being facilitated, but at present it is only a speculation. We do not know what it signifies.

Delmonte[3] has reviewed the literature on meditation and the electrical activity of the brain, using forms of meditation in

Verbal
Logical
Digital
Analytical
'Rational'

Non-verbal
Visuo-spatial
Synthetic
'Intuitive'

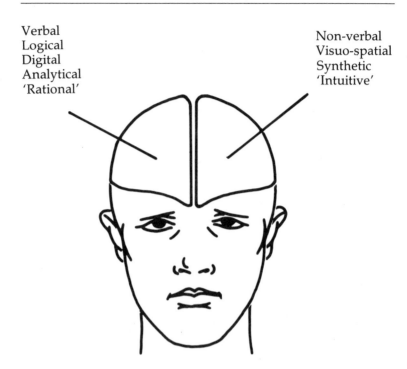

Differences in function and possibly style, between the left
and right halves of the brain.

which focussed attention plays a large part. TM is one such
technique. The overall findings include the fact that
meditation can produce decreased arousal (quieting of the
electrical activity of the brain). In addition, meditators more
readily demonstrate alpha and theta activity (signs of a state
of cortical relaxation), than non-meditators, even when they
are not meditating. This may be the product of meditation, or
it may be that those people who persist with, and benefit
from, meditation, already possessed those characteristics to
begin with. It is certainly possible that people with a capacity
for relaxed absorbed attention *are* alpha and theta-wave
producers and will also make successful meditators. This has
yet to be established.

While meditating, successful meditators show a stronger
orienting response, and a faster recovery, to stressful stimuli

than non-meditators. This underlines the beneficial effect of mental or cognitive quieting in coping with stress. Those able to achieve a state of relaxed, absorbed attention are not so affected by external stressors. Since those who can achieve this state in meditation can also produce electro-cortical signs of relaxation (alpha and theta waves) even when not meditating, the suggestion is that they have an enhanced ability to control stress reactions.

Meditation often begins with left cerebral hemisphere activity, which slowly gives way to right-hemisphere dominance; this is possibly because the monotonous repetition of the mantra blocks the more analytical and logical thought processes associated with the left hemisphere. During advanced meditation, right *and* left hemisphere activity is inhibited and this corresponds to a 'no thought' state. Delmonte reports that studies which suggest that synchrony between the hemispheres is a characteristic of meditation need to be replicated. In other words, the evidence is not yet clear.

The conclusion Delmonte comes to is that these fascinating changes in the brain's electrical activity (the significance of all of which are not yet understood fully) have been demonstrated in meditation, but may not be unique to it. They can also occur in hypnoidal states and in other forms of relaxation.

Studies on the Mantra

TM practitioners have suggested that the mantra causes synchrony as it sets up soothing and harmonious vibrations. Mantras are personal; once given by the teacher they are not to be used except for meditation and are not to be divulged. This makes studying the effects of them extremely difficult. It seems not to be the case that no two people are ever given the same mantra, but that there are groups of mantras which are felt suitable for different age-groups, or for people who live retiring and reclusive lives, or those who are out in the world. TM teachers hold that the wrong mantra, which someone might invent for themselves, or read in a book, can cause a lowering of mood and energy, as it is much more than just a sound on which to focus attention.

Morse et al[4] have conducted a study on the use of mantras. They looked at the effects of forty different words used as mantras. Some were meaningful English words, and some were Sanskrit and meaningless to the subjects. Subjects first rated the words as positive, neutral or negative, and they were then given a word from one category to meditate with. They reported that words rated as positive (such as love, sky) or neutral (such as shirrim, aum) were associated with pleasant body sensations like floating, warmth, or heaviness; on the other hand, negative-rated words (such as hate) induced negative body sensations like pain, cold, nausea or dizziness.

During meditation, subjects were observed and their body movements were recorded. Those using positive or neutral mantras produced the least frequent body movements; those using negative words produced the most frequent movements. Also, subjects rated the positive or neutral words as high in ease of induction of the meditation state, depth of meditation and euphoria. Here, then, is the suggestion that mantras do perhaps have special qualities, and that using the wrong words can result in a bad experience. However, some subjects went against the trend and reported that 'hate' produced more euphoria and deeper meditation than 'love', so individual differences are also a factor. Physiological measures showed no difference between the groups ultimately; all the measures suggested that, with practice, all subjects could attain a deep state of physiological relaxation, even when the subjective reports of subjects varied as to how pleasant they found the experience.

There are clearly three factors at work:

1) The subjective quality of the words, which have a bearing on the mental state;
2) Physiological relaxation, which is common to all mantras;
3) Some individual quirkiness, which went against the prevailing trend.

This seems to suggest that while the monotonous inner repetition of any word can trigger a dramatic, deep state of relaxation (because of the hypnotic nature of the activity, presumably), the required cognitive or mental changes sought in meditation may depend on something more subtle. The claim that mantras set up vibrations which lead to synchrony in the brain waves has not been scientifically established, but neither has it been firmly disproved. It is still open to question. Should it be proved, the significance of such synchrony would need to be established. The work remains to be done.

The Effects of TM

While the quality of much of the scientific work on TM has often been disappointing, and claims for its unique features remain largely unsubstantiated (although it holds its own as an effective relaxation technique), it is clear that hundreds of thousands of people have found something real and significant in the practice of TM. Peter Russell[5] reports his personal experience of becoming calmer, more stable, more self-assured, and getting things done more quickly and effectively. When some of his friends saw the change in him and began to practise TM too, he found his own experience confirmed in watching them. Harold Bloomfield[6] saw that 'meditating twice a day released the accumulated tensions of daily living and brought greater productivity and enjoyment'. As a practising psychiatrist, he then began to recommend TM to his patients.

One particular GP in Blackpool has been using transcendental meditation as a therapeutic technique for about six years and patients with migraine, premenstrual tension, anxiety leading to dependence on tranquillizers, nicotine and alcohol, have all benefitted greatly from the practice of meditation. Many have been able to come off all drugs. The doctor reports that when some returned later with a recurrence of symptoms this was associated with ceasing to practise the technique. On resumption the symptoms remitted. About a hundred patients have been treated in this way. Reports such as these are impressive. Whether the source of the healing is considered to come from deep within the self, or from some cosmic power, it is the conscious decision of the self to behave so as to reach it, and that is what makes it exciting. Coupled with that, the release from dependence on mind-altering substances such as alcohol, nicotine and minor tranquillizers can only be to the good.

Throll[7] has carried out a careful study comparing TM and progressive relaxation in terms of their physiological effects. He measured oxygen consumption, tidal volume (of lungs), respiration rate, heart-rate and blood-pressure in thirty-nine subjects. Then twenty-one learned TM and eighteen Jacobson's progressive relaxation. He tested them again on the physiological variables immediately after they learned the given technique,and again five, ten and fifteen weeks later. There were no significant differences between the groups before the experiment began and both groups displayed significantly lower metabolic rates while they were practising their given technique. However, the TM group showed more significant decreases during meditation and activity. Throll attributes this in part to the fact that the TM group spent more time on their technique. They were spending, on average, over four hours a week on it, while the progressive relaxers tended to spend thirty or forty minutes a week. Small wonder that the meditators got better results. The TM organization provided a one-to-one checking service to try to help them to keep up their time spent meditating. The progressive relaxers, with no such back-up and encouragement, tended to get bored and give up. Even so, they got good results; but not as impressive as those obtained by the TM group, who had a supportive organization to help them. There are surely lessons to be learned from this: motivation is all important; regular and consistent practice gets the best results.

Meditation certainly has all the benefits of relaxation training. The question is, does it have anything more? There is the argument that it is better for the cognitively-anxious than relaxation alone. There is also the added bonus of being part of a group with a shared philosophy, which could keep meditation going long after someone, taught to relax for a specific problem only, has given up. What we *know* about it is that it can be an excellent method of relaxation, and that its long-term use can have significant benefits for health. Meditators' heart-rates and blood-pressure respond more rapidly and recover more quickly than controls, when both are shown a stressful film. Long-term meditators are less aroused (i.e. have less autonomic arousal) than controls. Results such as these are probably also true for long-term relaxers, but that is not firmly established yet. As to whether there are some features of TM which are unique to it, and not shared by other relaxation techniques, that is not firmly established yet either, but it remains an exciting possibility.

References

1. Norton, G.R. and Johnson, W.E., 'A comparison of two relaxation procedures for reducing cognitive and somatic anxiety.' *Journal Behav. Ther. and Exptl. Psychiat.*, Vol. 14, No. 3, pp. 209–214, 1983.

2. Shapiro, D.H., 'Overview: clinical and physiological comparison of meditation with other self-control strategies.' *American Journal of Psychiatry*, 1982, 139(3), p. 267 on.

3. Delmonte, M.M., 'Electrocortical activity and related phenomena associated with meditation practice — a literature review.' *International Journal of Neuroscience*, 1984, Vol. 24, pp. 217-231.

4. Morse, D.R. et al, 'Meditation: an in-depth study.' *J. Am. Soc. Psychosom. Dent. Med.*, 1982, 29(5), pp. 1–96.

5. Russell P., *The Transcendental Meditation Technique: Introduction to Transcendental Meditation and the Teaching of the Maharishi Mahesh Yogi* (Routledge and Kegan Paul, 1977).

6. Bloomfield, H. et al, *Transcendental Meditation: How meditation can reduce stress* (Unwin Paperbacks, 1976).

7. Throll, D.A., 'Transcendental Meditation and relaxation: their physiological effects.' *J. Clin. Psychol.*, 1982, 38(3) pp. 522–30.

6. The Commonsense of Stress Management

Simple Measures

In the early chapters of this book, the 'fight or flight' syndrome was described. For primitive man it was crucial for personal survival, and nowadays we need it still — to keep us alert and constantly adapting to the complex world around us. It works for us unless it is overstretched and abused, in which case it may cause a variety of illnesses and disease states. The 'fight or flight' reaction is, of course, only one of our adaptive mechanisms, which range from the physiological to the cognitive or mental. It is perhaps in those mental processes, mediated by the cerebral cortex of the brain, that we see the supreme adaptive mechanisms. Our thoughts shape our behaviour, and we can consciously shape our own thoughts. We now also know that we can modify the triggering, speed and strength of some of our physiological reactions. Therefore the next step is to use this knowledge we have about ourselves to enhance good health, and to inhibit and change the destructive effects of stress on us.

In this book, some sources of stress and their effects have been identified, and a variety of methods of stress management has been explored. All of us meet some sorts of stress during a lifetime, and most of us get by somehow. Many people find their own way of dealing with the minor stresses of life. For some, using up a surge of adrenalin in physical activity seems to be the answer — after all, that is what adrenalin is there for, it may be said. A walk, a run, or a swim may be someone's formula for easing feelings of stress or tension. Participating in sports or games is another way of obtaining relaxation for many people, and a lot of them make a successful change to less strenuous forms of exercise, less dependent on youth and blooming health, as time goes on; trading in the squash and tennis rackets for golf clubs is one example of this.

There are also many homely routines, used by thousands of people, for relaxation. Listening to music, watching television, knitting, painting, gardening, making bread — the list of pleasant and enjoyable activities is as long as human ingenuity can make it. All these simple, and usually self-evolved, activities may be chosen by people for relaxation. We acknowledge that stresses build up during the day and take steps to restore ourselves to calm and equilibrium again. In a natural way, most of us manage our daily stresses. It is only when extra problems build up, or more intense no-way-out situations present themselves, that simple adaptive routines may be inadequate. Then we need to plan strategies, and to take the management of the problem on in an organized way.

Minimizing the Impact of External Stresses

Some stress-producing situations are predictable and we can plan ahead to minimize their impact on us. For example, things like driving tests, interviews and examinations are usually known about a long way in advance. All similar situations may produce a feeling of 'nerves' — in fact a reasonable amount of adrenalin may actually be helpful. It alerts and primes us for the activity and gives us some push. Any actor or actress will tell you that nerves are a necessary part of producing the performance. If you only suffer from an anticipatory tingle, then all you need to do before facing any sort of test is to ensure that you have had the amount of food and rest that your body normally needs and have had a reasonably quiet time beforehand, avoiding other extra stresses. If on the other hand, that sort of stress produces in you a range of symptoms such as shaking, sweating, disturbed sleep, 'knotted' stomach, or feelings of panic, then beginning a regular regime of quieting a month or so before facing the test, and giving yourself daily practice at it, may be necessary. It will also help to know that you are adequately rehearsed or prepared, and to have thought about what your next move will be should you pass or fail. Knowing yourself and your likely reactions and knowing in advance how you will cope with success or failure can take much of the fear out of examination-type situations.

If you have used minor tranquillizers in the past to help you in such situations, and using them has been successful, talk it over with your doctor if you want to change to a self-control regime of management; and give yourself time to try it out and get skilled at it first. Several different ways of achieving autonomic quieting have been described, and you will need to choose one to suit you. You could begin by trying a simple progressive relaxation technique. If it makes you feel deeply calm mentally and physically, perhaps it is the one you should stick with. If, on the other hand, your body is quietened by it, but your mind is still full of anxious, rushing thought, it may be that one of the more meditative techniques, such as TM or prayer, would suit you better. A few people feel extra tense when they lie down and try to relax, or find the physical exercises in Jacobson-style relaxation difficult for some reason. It may be that autogenic training is more suitable for them. For those for whom physical activity is a necessary part of quieting, Yoga or T'ai Ch'i could be the answer. It is clear from the literature that a whole range of different forms of relaxation can be very helpful. Just as our individual differences partly determine the way we react to stress, there are individual differences in how we will manage it.

Loss
Not all external stressors are as straightforward or as short-lived as an examination or a driving test. The more significant forms of stress, such as those involved in major loss or a bereavement, will clearly involve more than just keeping calm and sticking to a sensible, regular routine. Very often, a deep shock of that kind produces, first of all, a period of mental and emotional numbness. This 'frozen' state is probably self-protective; it is a time when the whole impact of the tragedy cannot be absorbed. It may be followed by a state in which only trivial details are attended to — again, focussing on the trivia happens because the person is not yet ready to face the whole important event. These are necessary parts of adjustment and do not require management beyond letting them run their course, and keeping extra demands to a minimum. As more of the impact of the event is faced, grief and sometimes depression may follow. Again these are natural consequences and do not usually need treatment.

Kindly support and undemanding care are the best kinds of help.

When this lowered mood lifts and reality is faced, then the bereaved person can be encouraged to take the initiative and begin to manage the situation, beginning with the basic things like adequate food and rest, and going on to examine their current state with all its good and bad points, and what their needs are now and for the future, and how they might be met. These can even be done as paper-and-pencil exercises, and are best carried out in a quiet, positive frame of mind. Here is where quieting can be useful. In a recent case, where a comparatively young mother had been left brain-damaged following a stroke, her husband and children were encouraged to explore the situation in this way, with a therapist. They made lists of the worst things about the situation, and were also encouraged to look for things which were good. The eldest daughter was able to say that she had matured through becoming 'mother'. Two of the younger children thought that the good things would be in the future, when mummy was better and able to be at home with them. This encouraged them all to look forward and make plans. Gains like these cannot usually be made by people under acute emotional stress; they come in periods of calm, and periods of calm can be self-generated.

Coping Skills

Barry Hopson[1] and his colleagues at Leeds University have developed training programmes to help people to use a range of coping skills in situations of personal stress. They have based their work on the life-changes studies of Holmes and Rahé (Chapter 2) and have evolved a questionnaire to help people undergoing transitional stress to identify coping skills they already possess, and highlight areas in which their skills need developing. The questionnaire is used in workshops where people have a chance to learn about and practise coping skills. Working with other people in learning situations can transform stress from a potentially destructive force into a vehicle for personal growth and gain. The questions cover areas like knowing yourself and the situation you are in, knowing people who can help, learning from similar past experiences, knowing how to look after yourself (including how to relax), letting go of the past, setting goals and making plans of action, and looking for the gains one has made. This kind of activity, which involves a detailed look at where you are and what you are, is obviously facilitated by working with professionals and others in a similar situation, but can also be a helpful home exercise.

Coping Skills Questionnaire

1. *Know yourself.*
a) Would I have chosen for this to have happened?
b) Am I proactive in new situations: do I take initiatives, have a purpose, as opposed to sitting back and waiting on events?
c) Do I know what I want from this new situation?
d) Do I know what I don't want from this new situation?
e) If I feel under stress do I know what I can do to help myself?

2. *Know your new situation.*
a) Can I describe the transition?
b) Do I know how I'm expected to behave?
c) Can I try out the new situation in advance?

3. *Know other people who can help;* do I have other people —
a) To depend on in a crisis?
b) To discuss concerns?
c) To feel close to — a friend?
d) Who can make me feel competent and valued?
e) Who can give me important information?
f) Who will challenge me to sit up and take a good look at myself?
g) With whom I can share good news and good feelings?
h) Who will give me constructive feedback?

4. *Learn from the past.*
a) Is there anything similar that has happened to me?
b) Can I identify what I did, which helped me to get through that experience?
c) Can I identify what I would have done differently?

5. *Look after yourself.*
a) Do I know how to use supportive self-talk?
b) Do I get regular exercise or have a personal fitness programme?
c) Am I eating regularly and wisely?

d) Do I know how to relax?
e) Am I keeping to a regular schedule?
f) Do I know my personal anchor points?
g) Do I give myself treats when under stress?
h) Do I have other people who will take care of me?
i) Can I survive?
j) Do I know when my low points are likely to be?

6. *Let go of the past.*
a) Do I easily let go of old situations?
b) Do I continually feel that this should not happen to me?
c) Do I know how to vent my anger constructively?

7. *Set goals and make action plans.*
a) Do I know how to set goals?
b) Do I know what my goals are for this transition and for my life in general?
c) Do I know how to make and implement action plans?
d) Do I know how to set priorities?
e) Do I know how to make effective decisions?
f) Do I know how to generate alternatives — because there is always an alternative?

8. *Look for gains you have made.*
a) Can I find one thing which is positive about this experience?
b) Can I list a variety of new opportunities that did not exist before, or that I would not have thought of previously?
c) Have I learnt something new about myself?

You could also try applying the following questions to your situation, preferably once you have learned and practised a relaxation technique. Write the answers down. Sleep on it and then read what you have written. It may be that turning the experience of stress into an exercise in thinking is the beginning of management. Here are the questions:

How long have I been feeling like this?
What (or who) started it?
What (or who) has kept it going?
What are the very specific things I find most stressful?
Are they objectively stressful, or is it my reaction?
Who can I trust to ask about it?
Can I change any of it? What?

What effect might that have?

If *I* change, what effect would that have on the situation or people in it? Suppose I stopped getting anxious or worried and was able to be very calm and rational — would it all change?

What is it that I want *most* to change?

If I could change that, can I tolerate the rest better?

If not, what else needs to change?

Are those changes possible?

Who can I go to for help?

You may be able to think of others. The important thing is to look at the problem rationally and calmly, rather than emotionally. Research has shown that we think less clearly when we are emotionally upset. We must learn how to be calm first, and then the management of the problem becomes possible. A teacher once said that she did all her best thinking in the bath. There was no telephone or television, there were no other people making demands. Her body was relaxed and her mind at peace. Archimedes presumably knew that feeling too, and how it facilitated creative thought.

In all the stress-managing techniques described in detail in this book under the general term 'quieting', the ability to enter a state of relaxed, focussed attention is central. It is obvious in things like progressive relaxation, autogenic training, and transcendental meditation, and in Yoga and T'ai Ch'i. It is also the 'central factor' which is probably crucial in autonomic conditioning using biofeedback. Some people can attain relaxed focussed attention easily and naturally, others have to work at it over a period of time and it may not come easily. It is, however, an important skill for personal health and well-being.

Ongoing Stress

One of the most damaging kinds of stress is that experienced by people trapped in an unhappy situation with no clear way out. Stress like this often involves personal relationships: within marriage, within the family, or at work. The single daughter coping alone with an increasingly senile parent; the violent marriage; the parent of a disturbed or heavily dependent handicapped child; the victim of the bully at school or difficult colleagues at work, are all obvious examples; chronic illness and pain can also produce similar problems. This is the sort of stress which can cause a person to begin each day with a feeling of dread, and end each day with trepidation about tomorrow. In situations like this, managing the internal response to stress is very important, but it will not necessarily change anything unless it is used in conjunction with thoughtful exploration and planning. Often, another person can facilitate this kind of exercise. It does not have to be a 'professional carer', but someone able to be concerned but not emotionally involved is most likely to be able to help. In addition, someone with knowledge of where to get practical help can be invaluable. (There is some information about where to get help in the last chapter of this book.)

Very often, the basic problem takes on a new perspective, even if it remains unchanged, when all the multitude of difficulties associated with it are looked at calmly, and some are cleared out of the way. For example, a patient suffering chronic pain was coping very well with her condition, and keeping her pain levels low with the help of relaxation practised on a regular basis. However, one of the problems associated with her pain was that she was unable to tend her garden, or carry shopping; and as the weeds and grass grew, she was unable to face her neighbours in the neat road in which she lived and became distressed and isolated, with poorer pain control. When she was put in touch with a vounteer group who sent someone on a regular basis to tidy the garden, she felt more in command of things again and was able to organize her shopping in conjunction with one of her daughters who had a car. An elderly lady living with a *very* elderly and domineering parent, whose awkwardness had brought her to the brink of a nervous illness, improved dramatically when twice-weekly day care was arranged for the parent, and holidays were organized for them separately. She needed breathing space and time to herself, not medical treatment.

Many of these practical difficulties can be dealt with by self-help groups or voluntary organizations, or by people like health visitors, social workers or marriage guidance counsellors. No-one should feel afraid to ask for help: it is good preventive care to step in before the crisis leads to illness, which can be a long and difficult thing to cure.

Some people prefer to help than be helped. In some cases, it is possible to 'trade' skills or services. One patient, unable to do housework because of severe back problems, traded cake-making for hoovering. She made wonderful light sponges, a skill her neighbour lacked. The solution was that the back-patient baked for both of them, while the neighbour hoovered for both. In another case, two young mothers gave each other an afternoon off each week; one had both babies while the other had time to herself. When life was centred on small village communities, these things were commonplace. Now, we may need to plan them consciously, but they still work. In my own area there are successful groups providing support and care for those with agoraphobia, for the parents of twins, for the relatives and friends of neurological patients, and the parents of handicapped children, to name only a few. There are also many churches with their own groups. On a less formal basis there are shared transport arrangements for schoolchildren, babysitting circles, a grannysitting service, and dog-walkers. In most cases, no money changes hands — goodwill is the currency. All these schemes were started by people with needs finding each other. Someone took the initiative in each case and an apparently insoluble problem became a thing to be managed.

Most of the examples quoted here involve simple, practical solutions. No one solution answers all the problems, but each one removes one or more sources of potential stress.

It is easy to understand the inter-relationship between our mental, emotional and bodily states — almost instinctively we know that adequate rest, exercise and nutrition make us feel better in spirit as well as body. We know how badly we cope with daily life when we are overtired or unwell. It should not be hard, therefore, to take the next step, and to understand that a regular quieting routine can enhance not only good bodily health, but mental and emotional well-being. It needs to be a regular rather than an occasional emergency measure when feelings of tension are excessive. Quieting responses should be part of management rather than first-aid.

References

1. Hopson, B., 'Transition: understanding and managing personal change' in *Psychology and People: A Tutorial Text*, Ed. A.J. Chapman and A. Gale (Macmillan Press, 1982).

7. Taking Responsibility

Moderation

Combatting stress is an important part of preventive and curative health care, and it cannot be achieved passively. To restate a proposition from the beginning of this book — taking more responsibility for our own health is crucial to the modern management of many diseases and disorders. This is not to say, however, that we should reject all the excellent help available from contemporary medicine and surgery, and

. . . marvellous new diet! Carrots and lettuce juice.

go it alone. We need to be well-informed, to know when and where to get outside help, and to temper enthusiasm for self-help with doses of moderation and common sense. There is no panacea. Fanatical devotion to the all-health-giving power of aerobics, carrot juice or regular relaxation is misguided. Any or all of those things may be beneficial as part of a planned health-care regime, but no diet, exercise, or quieting regime has magic properties. In particular, inner harmony will not be achieved by most of us by mortifying the flesh in excessive mental or physical exercise, or esoteric diets. The old Greek adage 'moderation in all things' is not to be despised and should guide those taking the initiative for more of their own health care.

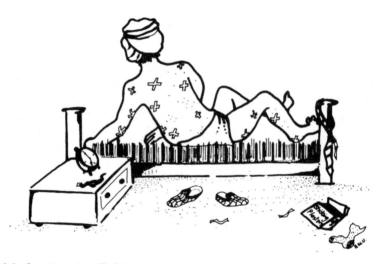

Moderation in all things . . .

Understanding
The aim of this book has been, first, to try to unravel the vague and yet complicated word 'stress', and to explain some of the known physiological and psychological effects of stress. It seemed important to do that before getting on to the main part of the book, which is about techniques for managing stress, for the following reason: health care is changing, and there is now the beginning of a real emphasis on prevention in medicine and its allied arts and sciences. This revolution — for it certainly is that dramatic a change — depends very

largely on people taking more responsiblity for their own health. This cannot be accomplished in ignorance. A book describing two alternative relaxation techniques on a 'try it and see' basis is not much better than a label on a pill bottle saying 'take one when tense'. We must understand why something is good for us or bad for us, and understand it in some depth, or why should we let it impinge on us at all? In a clinical practice, time taken to explain why anxiety produces breathlessness or 'butterflies', or why our thoughts race but get us nowhere when we are tense or upset, is time well spent. No-one can begin to manage a situation which they do not fully understand.

This book, then, was conceived as a practical aid to stress management. It could be used on its own by someone seeking to deal with personal stresses. However, professional help should be sought, and is readily available, where the problems are too much to tackle alone.

If you are already being helped by your GP or hospital specialist it is very unwise to abandon that source and decide to 'go it alone' impulsively. Talk over self-help techniques with your doctor. He may refer you on to a clinical psychologist, who will work from a district general hospital, psychiatric hospital, or be community-based. Some are in health centres working alongside general practice doctors. Other health care professionals, such as occupational therapists and practice nurses, may also be trained to teach relaxation techniques. Your doctor will also know if counselling is available in your area. Some counselling is free, or you may be asked to contribute what you can afford. Some counsellors work in the private sector.

Drugs

If you are being treated for anxiety or stress with drugs, do not just stop them without consulting your doctor. It may be that you need to reduce them slowly, and this is best done under medical supervision. If you are being treated for serious nervous or mental disturbance with one of the major tranquillizers (such as phenothiazines), you should not stop them in favour of, say, meditation. Such conditions are complicated long-term disorders in which stress is not an established factor. Some people suffering from these disorders may find techniques like meditation exacerbate their symptoms. Like anyone else, they will benefit from regular, pleasant exercise and healthful relaxation, but would be unwise to experiment further.

Where To Find Help
Help for health
Some Regional Health Authorities have 'Help for Health' Services, which carry a wide range of information about health matters, including lists of contacts for self-help groups. Again, your family doctor or local Health Education Council will know how you can get in touch with them. One good example of an organization which helps people overcome anxiety is Phobic Action (see page 109 for its address).

Self-taught relaxation
For those who want to embark on a regular programme of relaxation, but do not feel that they need professional or other outside help, it is possible to follow the regime given in Chapter 4 (see page 66). Learning to relax deeply comes more easily to some people than others. It is like learning a musical instrument — regular daily practice achieves results over time. Many people find it easier to use taped instructions. You could record those given in the book onto a cassette to play for yourself, or get someone with an especially soothing or pleasant voice to do it for you. There are several good relaxation tapes on the market, too, which are advertised in national publications as well as some very good music tapes designed to aid relaxation.

Autogenic training
Autogenic training is becoming increasingly available. Again, ask your GP or Help for Health service if it is available as part of the Health Service in your area. In the private sector, The Centre for Autogenic Training (see page 109 for address) will send you a list of qualified teachers if you send them a stamped addressed envelope. Prices for an eight-week training course will be about £150 (1985 figures).

Transcendental meditation
Many large cities have a Transcendental Meditation Centre, if you feel that TM is the technique you would prefer to try. If you have any difficulty making contact, you could write to the

national office — the address is on page 109.

T'ai Ch'i
If you would like to try T'ai Ch'i as a way of combining relaxed focussed attention and gentle exercise you may find teachers of the technique where oriental martial arts are taught. The movements, although gentle and graceful, have been evolved from ancient self-defence arts. There are clubs in many towns and the British T'ai Ch'i Ch'uan Association (see address on page 109) will give details of classes nationwide.

Yoga
Yoga is often taught as an evening class or day class, as part of Adult Education or Keep Fit. You may see it publicized in your local library, or you can ask the librarian for information about classes. Alternatively, you can contact the Iyengar Yoga Institute — the address is on page 109.

Life Skills
At the simplest level, build in time for walking, swimming, music — any of those pleasant, relaxing activities which are so easy to jettison when the pressures build up. Time spent in restoring your body's equilibrium, and your mind's sense of calm and control, is time very well spent, and it is best spent on a regular basis, rather than as an occcasional emergency measure when feelings of tension are running high. Quieting responses should be part of management rather than first aid. At the very least, they are pleasant and calming, but that is clearly only a small part of the story. Using them as part of stress-management can be life-enhancing and, for some people, life-saving.

For example, the latest piece of research to hand (Patel et al[1]) has shown that relaxation can reduce the risk of coronary heart disease. Patel and colleagues found 192 women and men aged thirty-five to sixty-four with two or more risk factors on screening. The risk factors were blood-pressure higher than 140/90, raised plasma cholesterol, and a current smoking habit of more than ten cigarettes a day. The subjects were randomly allocated to one of two groups. Both groups were given health education leaflets containing advice to stop smoking, reduce animal fats in the diet, and on the importance of reducing blood-pressure. In addition, the treatment group had eight weeks of one hour a week group sessions of breathing exercises, relaxation and meditation, and teaching about managing stress. An earlier study had shown that at eight weeks and eight months follow-up there was significantly greater reduction in blood-pressure in the treatment group, compared with the other group. The current study showed that those differences were maintained at four year follow-up. At four years, more subjects in the other (control) group reported having had angina and treatment for hypertension. The incidence of ischaemic heart disease, fatal myocardial infarction, or electrocardiographic evidence of ischaemia was significantly greater in the control group. (Ischaemia and angina both occur because the blood supply to the heart has become inadequate.)

The implications of a study such as this are profound. The authors calculated that, four years after the study, the treatment group has a twelve per cent reduction in risk of coronary heart disease. This was four years after a simple eight-hour programme of relaxation, training and stress management teaching. As this book shows, these techniques are very simple, and require only time and some careful thought. They have an impact not only on risk factors in coronary heart disease, but on many other aspects of health. Stress can be a killer, but it need not kill *you*. It can produce a range of bad things, from unhappiness to ill-health, or you can learn to manage external stressors and internal stress responses, and stay happier and healthier.

Relaxation is a skill for life.

References

1. Patel, C. et al., 'Trial of relaxation in reducing coronary risk: four year follow-up.' British Medical Journal, Vol. 290, 13 April 1985, 1103–1106.

Useful Addresses

The British T'ai Ch'i Ch'uan Association
7 Upper Wimpole Street
London W1
(Tel. 01-935 8444)

The Centre for Autogenic Training
101 Harley Street
London W1N 1DF

The Iyengar Yoga Institute
223A Randolph Avenue
London W9
(Tel. 01-624 3080)

National Capital of the Age of Enlightenment
Maharishi International College
Roydon Hall
Seven Mile Lane
East Peckham
Kent TN12 5NH

New World Cassettes
Freepost F2
Twickenham TW1 1BR
Will provide a list of music tapes designed to aid relaxation.

Phobic Action
8 Westrow Drive
Barking
Essex IG11 9BH

Further Reading

J.D. Adams, J. Hayes and B. Hopson, *Transition: Understanding and Managing Personal Change* (Martin Robertson, 1976).

T.T. Liang, *T'ai Ch'i Ch'uan for Health and Self-defence* (Vintage Books, 1977).

P. Russell, *The Transcendental Meditation Technique: Introduction to Transcendental Meditation and the Teaching of the Maharishi Mahesh Yogi* (Routledge and Kegan Paul, 1978).

Peta Whaley, *Yoga: A Beginner's Guide* (Bell and Sons, 1974).

Index